MW00610056

# Arabic Religious Rhetoric

## The Radical Saudi Sheikhs

### A Reader

Peter D. Molan

# Arabic Religious Rhetoric
## The Radical Saudi Sheikhs
### A Reader

Peter D. Molan

2002
Dunwoody Press

*Arabic Religious Rhetoric: The Radical Saudi Sheikhs: A Reader*



First Edition 1997
Second Impression 2002



All inquiries should be directed to:
Dunwoody Press
6564 Loisdale Ct., Suite 800
Springfield, VA 22150, USA

ISBN: 1-881265-38-2
Library of Congress Catalog Card Number: 97-069479
Printed and bound in the United States of America

# Contents

# Preface and Acknowledgments

This book is intended primarily as a language learning device for the intermediate or advanced student of modern formal Arabic, but we hope that it may be, as well, of interest to a wider audience based on the inherent importance of the material it presents. It began as a teacher's personal, classroom project. It would have remained only that, and never seen the light of day as a publishable work, had others not seen its potential.

With the encouragement of colleagues the project described below was brought to the attention of Dunwoody Press. It is their interest that has made publication possible. Dunwoody brought me into contact with their staff, to whom the transcriptions presented below are, initially, due and without whom the project could not have proceeded. Together, we wish to express our thanks and appreciation for Dunwoody's support which has brought our endeavors to fruition. Many thanks too to those who are not named here but without whom the work would have been stillborn at the outset. Thanks to Professor Amin Bonna of Georgetown University whose comments in the first stages of the project were very useful and much appreciated. Special thanks to Nadia Dimitry, Marti Hawkins and Jack Jones who proofread the whole manuscript. Its shortcomings, are all my own.

Peter D. Molan, Ph.D.
Baltimore, MD.
30 August 1997

# Introduction

## On the Project

On September 28, 1992, an article in the *Washington Post* piqued the interest of many observers of the Middle East (both professional and lay) including my own. The article, entitled "Conservative Clergy Attack Saudi Government," brought to our attention a new set of players on Saudi Arabia's political stage.

The article described the contents of the so called "Memorandum of Advice" which some one-hundred fifty religious scholars had sent to Fahd Bin $^{C}$Abd al-$^{C}$Aziz, the reigning monarch of the Kingdom of Saudi Arabia. These scholars objected to a number of the Saudi government's policies and called upon the King to change them. The article mentioned that the scholars were using audio tapes to spread their ideas among the population of Saudi Arabia at large.

The scholars involved were, by and large, educated in state sponsored institutions of religious learning and were employed in those self same universities or in other government sanctioned mosques or schools. They represented, in that respect, a distinctly new manifestation of political opposition within the Kingdom.

Earlier oppositionist tendencies within the Saudi regime had been much more circumspect in their criticisms. Actual opposition had come from circles clearly outside of the establishment, as had Juhayman al-$^{C}$Utaiba who occupied the Haram al-Sharif in Mecca militarily in 1979.

The use of tape recordings was also new and, of course, reminiscent of Ayatullah Khomeini's methods in Iran. The desire to know more about these individuals and their thinking was irresistible.

I began trying to follow their story in the American, European and Arab press and in such reporting as came into my ken. The following comments are based on a file of some two hundred articles and reports as well as scholarly articles by Dekmejian, al-Rasheed, and Savin which have appeared in the *Middle East Journal*, *Current History*, and the *Middle East Quarterly*, respectively.

I was, however, particularly interested in hearing, first hand, what these "radically conservative" Sheikhs had to say on their tapes. Accordingly, I asked friends in Saudi Arabia to procure a sample of the tapes in question for me. They sent me a collection of fourteen such tapes.

In the following introductory pages, I will provide the barest of background and biographical data on the speakers, selections of whose "sermons," "lessons," and "lectures" -- along with transcriptions and translations -- form the body of the book. As regards the tapes themselves, I have tried to choose selections from the total collection which will represent the views of their authors, on the subjects in question, fairly. On the other hand, I have also chosen what seem to me to be the most interesting elements; doing so has tended to distill out the commonplace (and moderate) and to concentrate (or "intensify") the controversial features of the materials.

I have chosen to present selections on the topics of politics, the status of women, and religious tolerance (among others) which are among the hottest issues in the current cultural dialogue between secularists and the religious, in general, and between "Westerners" and "Islamists" in particular. In doing so I have edited out quotations from the Qur'an and *Hadith* and from poetry (both classical and contemporary) which so prominently characterize the tapes. I have also edited out what I deem to be digressions peripheral to the issues at hand, in order to get down to what I see as the heart of the matter. I have done so in the full realization that I have cut out what the believing Muslim will view as most important -- the Qur'anic citations. I do so with apologies and in all humility, but I do so in the conviction that this collection of taped materials offers students of contemporary Arabic a major opportunity through which to acquaint themselves with a realm of discourse that is of growing importance but which has, heretofore, received but little attention from the perspectives of either language study *per se* or discourse analysis.

It must also be noted that these preachers are angry and passionate men. Their discourse is unrestrained and contains language which may well offend those who adhere to other systems of belief. The reader must be forewarned and perhaps take into account the Sheikhs' own sense of being at mortal risk.

## Background Notes on the Sheikhs

Arabia is the site of the advent of Islam through the Prophet Muhammad's preaching and governance. It was also the site of the celebrated "School of Medina" associated with the teaching of Malek Bin Anas and the earliest stages in the development of Islamic legal, theological and linguistic study. Though it had lost its centrality over the centuries, centers of religious learning had never disappeared from the Peninsula, and under the Sa$^{c}$ud family, religious education had taken a new turn with the foundation of the Shari$^{c}$ah College in Mecca which dates back to the 1920s and 30s. A new stage in the development of contemporary Islamic studies began with the foundation of the Islamic University in Medina in 1961. The trend continued in 1976 with the establishment of the Imam Muhammad Ibn Sa$^{c}$ud University in Riyadh and saw the expansion of Mecca's Shari$^{c}$ah College to become the Umm al-Qura University in 1982. Since then, the Imam Muhammad University has opened branches in five provincial cities.

This spread of university style centers of religious learning arose, to a not inconsiderable extent, in response to the diffusion of Western style scientific and technical education (which must in turn acknowledge its own debt to the Classical Arab-Islamic mosque-madrasah) and to the increase in study abroad among young Saudi Arabians.

It must be recalled that the turn towards the West was motivated by a Saudi desire to gain technical mastery of its own economic destiny. That turn, however, came at a time during which Western youth was rebelling against the internal contradictions, constraints, and conflicts of their own societies, a rebellion associated with the civil rights movement, the "sexual revolution," and ultimately, the Viet Nam war.

Saudi religious leaders of that generation perceived a threat to Islam in an increasing impact upon their society by the West. They appealed to their government to establish new institutions of religious learning and to encourage involvement with them as a response to the danger. The government responded positively, as described above, and by the eighties, a new generation of religious scholars had begun to graduate and take positions in their own expanding colleges and universities as well as in local mosques and schools.

While respecting their teachers, at whose head is Sheikh $^{c}$Abd al-$^{c}$Aziz Bin Baz -- Saudi Arabia's Chief Mufti, many of the new generation of scholars believe that the dangers seen by their teachers have grown even beyond their elders' capacity to forestall. Those dangers came to the crisis stage during the 1990-91 Gulf War. Their "Memorandum of Advice" and taped appeals for a new Islamic activism within Saudi Arabia were their responses.

Among the most active of the signatories to the "Memorandum of Advice," and among the most prolific producers of tapes, are Safar Bin $^{c}$Abd al-Rahman al-Hawali, $^{c}$A'ed al-Qarni, Salman al-$^{c}$Awdah, and Naser al-$^{c}$Umar. The collection of tapes upon which this book is based contains sermons and lectures by the first three.

Safar al-Hawali was born in 1953. He received an MA in theology from the Umm al-Qura University in 1979 and was later appointed "lecturer" at the Islamic University of Madina's "Religious Fundamentals" College. He completed his PhD at the Umm al-Qura University in 1987 graduating first in his class. He came to prominence in 1990 when he publicly opposed the invitation of U.S. forces into the Kingdom.

Salman al-$^{c}$Awdah was born in 1956 in Buraydah. He received his MA from the Imam Muhammad University in 1987 and taught at his university's "Shari$^{c}$ah College" in his home town.

$^{c}$A'ed al-Qarni is somewhat younger. He is regarded, however, as the most polished speaker of his peers. He is an accomplished poet and a regular contributor to the daily newspaper *al-Madina*. He has been a lecturer at the Abha branch of the Imam Muhammad University. Like Sheikhs Safar and Salman, Sheikh $^{c}$A'ed knows the West from personal travel to it.

It must be noted that the Saudi government moved, in 1993-94, to suppress the activities of their radical young Sheikhs. Their tapes are no longer openly available, and all three are now, or have been until recently, in jail despite the best efforts of Saudi human rights organizations in London. The government has been accused of abusing them while in detention.

## On the Format, Style and Quality of the Tapes

It is my intention to allow the Saudi Sheikhs to speak for themselves on topics which I categorize as "Political Theory and Democracy," "Internal Division," "Foreign Policy and Relations with the United States," "The Status of Women," "Religious Tolerance and Human Rights," "Western Aims," and "Solutions." I append a segment on "Audience Reactions." Since, however, I have chosen only *selections* from the Sheikhs' lectures, and since my listener/reader may be denied the opportunity to hear or read any of the cassettes as a whole, I include here, as introductory material, a brief description of, and recorded sample characteristic of, the format and style of the lectures in hand.

### Format

Each tape opens with an announcement from the tape manufacturer; that announcement may be followed by a brief segment of formal Qur'anic recitation. The featured speaker is then heard introducing his "lecture" or "lesson" (the terms seem to be used interchangeably) usually with a brief خطبة in praise of the Prophet Muhammad in rhymed prose. The speaker then turns to the topic at hand.

### Style

The lectures appear not to be scripted. Hesitations, mid-sentence corrections, digressions, repetitions, and shifts in subject, tense and mood all suggest extemporaneous speech. The speakers do refer to books, documents and letters, passages of which they often read out. The facility with which they cite the Qur'an, the Hadith, and both classical and contemporary poetry, upon which to ground their arguments or with which to embellish their lectures, however, suggests that they either work from notes or are true literary masters.

In terms of the classical-colloquial continuum of contemporary Arabic discourse, the speakers are self conscious about maintaining a high level of classicism. Only rarely do they switch into the dialect. When they do, they seem to seek a specific stylistic effect. In this regard, note especially Sheikh Safar's comments about the style of the letter in question in Selection 6 below and his use of the dialectal والله ينطيك العافية rather than the standard يُعْطيكَ in Selection 5.

The lectures are obviously recorded before "live" audiences; in some cases the specific venue of the talk is mentioned as in Selection 4. Occasionally the audience is heard to respond to a point which the Sheikh makes, as in Selection 5 (here with its laughter at the Sheikh's joke); less often there is a brief exchange between the speaker and a member of the audience. Far more commonly, however, what we hear is a straight lecture. In two cases, the speaker responds to questions, but they are previously collected, written questions rather than questions from the floor.

## Quality

The voice quality of the tapes is somewhat variable. Generally, the sound technicians who have produced the recordings have done a good, or at least acceptable, job. None of the tapes is, however, recorded in a studio or concert hall setting, and the problems of "live" recording in such venues as mosques and lecture halls are evident. Echo is a recurring phenomenon, though in no instance does it become overly intrusive. Occasionally there are variations in recording level. In at least one case, the voice quality is noticeable "fuzzy," and there are not infrequent, though brief, gaps resulting in a missed word or two. No attempt has been made to improve the original voice quality; the recordings are presented as they appear "off the shelf."

## An Example of the Format and Style of the Saudi Sheikhs' Lectures

### Selection 1

#### *The Corporate Introduction*

بسم الله الرحمن الرحيم    أخي المسلم أختي المسلمة تسجيلات المسلم
السمعية والمرئية ترحب بكم وتقدم ...

In the name of God the Merciful, the Compassionate: my brother Muslim, my sister Muslim, "Muslim Audio-Visual Recordings" welcomes you and presents...

### Selection 2

#### *Tajwid*

سبحان الذي أسري بِعبده ليلا من المسجد الحرام إلى المسجد الاقصا
الذي باركنا حوله لنُرِيَه من آياتنا إنّه هو البسميع البصير

Glory be to He who sped His servant by night from the "Holy Mosque" to the "Furthest Mosque" (the precincts of which We have blessed) so We might show him some of Our signs. Verily He is the All-hearing, the All-seeing.*

* Qur'an 17:1.

### Selection 3

#### *The Speaker's* خطبة *

بسم الله الرحمن الرحيم إن الحمدلله نحمده ونستعينه ونستغفره
ونستهديه ونعوذ بالله من شرور أنفسنا ومن سيئات أعمالنا من
يهده الله فلا مضل له ومن يُضلل فلا هادي له واشهد أن لا إله إلا الله
وأشهد أن محمدا عبده ورسوله صلى الله عليه وعلى آله وصحبه وسلم
تسليماً كثيراً

In the name of God the Merciful, the Compassionate. All praise be to God. We praise Him, and we seek His assistance; we seek His forgiveness, and we seek His guidance. We take refuge in God from the evil of our souls and from the sins of our acts. He whom God guides, there is none to lead him astray; and he whom He sends astray, he has none to guide him aright. I testify that there is no god but God, and I testify that Muhammad is his servant and apostle. May God send down His blessings upon him, upon his family and upon his Companions, and may He grant him the utmost peace.

* The term خطبة [khutbah] refers to the Friday "sermon" in a mosque but also to the rhymed prose introduction which must necessarily open any Islamic book or speech (including a Friday "sermon" *per se*) regardless of its subject matter. The khutbah has a specific form; it praises God, invokes His aid in the venture at hand, and honors the Prophet Muhammad, as in the case in hand.

## Selection 4

### *The Speaker's Introduction of His Subject*

أما بعد إخوة الإيمان حملة العقيدة السلام عليكم ورحمة الله وبركاته . عنوان هذا الدرس <<صرخة فتاة .>> فتاة صرخت برسالة سوف أقرأها وأعلق عليها والله المستعان . ولكن قبل هذا ألتمس إليكم التقارب ... أن تتقاربوا حتى يتمكن الإخوة الذين هم خارج المسجد من دخول المسجد . تقاربوا أيها الجمع الكريم فكم بقربكم يشرق التوفيق والأمل لقاؤكم ... لقاؤنا بكم . للعين قرتها . في ساحكم تذكر الاخيار والرسل

Now thereafter: Brothers in faith, bearers of the true doctrine, may peace and the mercy of God and His blessings be upon you. The title of this lesson is "A Girl's Cry." A girl has cried out in a letter which I will read and comment upon, and God is the One whose assistance is sought. But, before that, I ask you to come close, to approach so that the brothers who are outside of the mosque will be able to enter the mosque. Come close O you honorable gathering, for how greatly, through your proximity, will success and hope brighten your meeting ... our meeting with you?* Every eye has its delight; in your tribunals the best and the prophets are mentioned.†

* Though he gives "meeting" the nominative case, it should presumably be the object of the verb and in the accusative.

† This would appear to be a poetic citation, but I have been unable to identify it.

## Selection 5

### *Stylistics -- the Use of Colloquial Arabic and Audience Reactions*

بالمناسبة الشيخ على طنطاوي في كتاب ذكرياته يذكر قصة من قلب المفاهيم وهي دعابة فكاهة يقول «في سوريا كان عندهم طبيب وفد عليه شابان قويان فلاحان مزارعان الواحد منهم يهد الجدار بعضلاته ومعهم ام عجوز تدب دبيباً فشكت آلامها على الطبيب فأعطاهم الطبيب قارورة فيها علاج قال تخضونها ( والضمير ما بيّن هي القارورة والعجوز) تخضونها خضاً وتهزونها هزاً ثم تُسقونها ملعقة في الصباح وملعقة في المساء فذهب الذكيان العبقريان إلى البيت واستلما العجوز يخضونها في الصباح ويخضونها في المساء فإذا خضوها وهزوها هزاً حتى تولول من رأسها إلى قدميها أسقوها ملعقة فإذا أتى المساء خضوها خمسة عشر يوم تصور يخضونها في الصباح ويخضونها في المساء ويهزونها في الصباح ويهزونها في المساء كانت تمشي وفي الأخير أصبحت معطلة في البيت ذهبوا إلى الطبيب بعد خمسة عشر يوم قالوا والله لا ينطيك العافية كانت أمنا تمشي على الأرض والأن أصبحت محرولة في البيت قال ولمَ ؟ قالوا خضضناها خمسة عشر يوماً ومرضت قال خض الله رؤوسكم أقول خضوا القارورة لاتخضوا العجوز.» فأنا مقصدي هذه الليلة ألا تخضوا المرأة إنما المرأة تخضكم

Apropos of that, Sheikh 'Ali Tantawi, in his memoirs, relates a story of profound wisdom. It's a joke, a funny story. He says: "In Syria, they had a doctor to whom two strong, peasant, farming youths came along. Either one of them could knock down a wall because of his muscles. Now, with them was their old mother crawling along like a snake. She made complaint of her pains to the doctor. The doctor gave them a bottle in which was some medicine; he said: "shake'r up ( but the pronoun isn't clear; it could be the bottle or the old woman), shake'r up well and joggle'r up well and give'r a spoonful in the morning and another spoonful in the evening. So these two bright geniuses went home and grabbed the old woman shaking her up in the morning and shaking her in the evening. And, when they had shaken her hard and joggled her well, until she was trembling* from head to foot, they poured her a spoonful. When evening came they shook her for fifteen days. Just imagine them shaking her in the morning and shaking her in the evening and joggling her in the morning and joggling her in the evening. She had been walking but finally she became incapacitated in the house. They went to the doctor after fifteen days; they said: "May God not grant you good health†. Our mother used to walk the earth, but now, she's come to be restricted to the house." He said: "And, why's that?" They said: "we shook her up for fifteen days and she got sick." He said: "May God shake up your heads. I was telling you to shake up the bottle, not for you to shake up the old woman." My aim this evening is not that you should shake up woman but that woman should shake you up.

* The usual meaning of ولول is "wail, lament"; this translation follows the context.

† Note the intentional use of the dialectal form here.

## Selection 6

### *Further Introductory Remarks on Style*

أما هذه فهي رسالتها والله الشاهد . كتبتها ورمزت اسمها وأنا لاأذكر الرمز ولكني أقرأ الرسالة . وعفواً قد يكون في أسلوبها هي ركاكة في بعض النواحي . لا في أسلوبي . أعاذني الله . وأعاذها الله. لكن في أسلوبي أنا أقرأها كما سمعت بعض الكلمات العامية أو ربما بعض التحريفات اللغوية والنحوية لكن للأمانة أقرأها كما سمعتها .

Now this is her letter, as God is my witness. She wrote it and alluded to her name. I won't mention the allusion, but I will read the letter. Excuse me; there may be, in her own style, some weakness in certain respects. It's not in my style. May God protect me! May God protect her. But, in my own style, I'll read it as I heard it -- some colloquial words or perhaps some linguistic or grammatical mistakes, but for fidelity, I'll read it as I heard it.

## On the Translations

In translating, I have aimed at an English prose that will, to the extent possible, reflect the structure of the Arabic as heard. That aim is meant to assist the Arabic speaking student without overburdening the text with grammatical notes. Relative clauses, "circumstantial" clauses, "topic comment" sentences,* etc. are all rendered in a fairly literal manner and should, therefore, alert the student to their existence when the Arabic structure may be difficult for the beginning student to identify. Notes on cultural issues, and on vocabulary not found in Hans Wehr's *A Dictionary of Modern Standard Arabic* , are appended as needed.

On the other hand, I hope that the translations will be more than a student's "trot." I hope that the translations will give a clear and comprehensible rendering of the Arabic for those whose interest lies in the content of the lessons rather than their language *per se*.

I have not, however, tried to formalize the spoken nature of the Sheikhs' discourse. I have tried to convey the informal register of the language used in these lectures and lessons by using English contractions, idioms and slang where it has seemed appropriate to do so. I have also tried to make the inevitable ellipses and parenthetical comments within parenthetical statements of spoken language comprehensible -- mostly by careful punctuation, sometimes by reinterpolating previously used terms to maintain coherence. Finally, I have tried to deal with the problem of obscure pronominal reference so common to Arabic style, through the reinterpolation of the referred-to nouns for obscure pronouns. My interpolations are in square brackets [ ]. All other parenthetical symbols refer to parenthetical comments in the original. I use ellipses [...] to indicate a longish pause or hesitation in the original talk and not an omission of text. Each selection presented is complete; all omissions fall between the selections. The numbering of the selections is arbitrarily introduced to facilitate identification and no such segmentation is to be found in the original recordings.

It must be noted that I have not been able to track down every point on which a note might be appropriate, and a few references remain obscure to me. I have commented on some dialectalisms that seemed particularly noteworthy but not on every occurrence of such features of speech.

As regards the transliteration of Arabic terms and names into the Latin alphabet, I have used ['] to represent the Arabic همـزة and [$^{C}$] to represent the Arabic [ع], but I have marked neither emphatic consonants nor long vowels. In virtually all cases, the Arabic text is close at hand for those who need such information.

* A special note on "topic comment" sentences may be in order. They do exist in English but are rare. Jane Austin, in *Persuasion* -- for instance, said: "The Wallaces, she had pleasure in observing them." That is, "She had pleasure in observing the *Wallaces* " [rather than the Jones]. Note that an element of an underlying, basic sentence (here "the Wallaces") is moved to the beginning, or "head," of the "topic-comment" sentence, and its original place is marked by a pronoun which agrees with that "head noun." The "head noun" has become the "topic" which the following independent clause "comments" upon. While rare in English, this sentence structure is the principle way of emphasizing a particular part of a sentence in Arabic. I have, therefore, tended to preserve it in translation, and it will be encountered very frequently below, not, I hope, to the distress of my readers.

# Chapter One

# On Politics

## Introduction

As many moderate Arab observers (both Muslim and secular of many nationalities) have pointed out, "Islamists" criticize current social conventions and political systems harshly; they then call for the establishment of "Islamic" political regimes but without defining what they mean. The common slogans are "Islam is the answer," "no constitution save the Qur'an and the Sunnah," and "establish the Shari'ah." But "What," such self described Muslim moderates as Egypt's Fu'ad Zakariya ask, "is the program?" "What are the details?" None are offered they claim.

That claim is borne out in the sample of tapes here being explored. Nowhere is there any description of what an Islamic political regime might be like. Comments on political theory, other than somewhat veiled assertions that current political organization is unacceptable, occur only twice.*

One passage takes the form of Safar al-Hawali's categorical rejection of "democracy" coupled with an expressed willingness to participate in an electoral process in order to achieve Islamist ends. The statement occurs in a tape entitled "The Meaning of Bin Baz's Statement." In it, Sheikh Safar would seem to justify the fears often expressed in Algeria that free elections and an Islamic electoral victory would mean no more than "one man one vote one time."

His reference to participating in a democratic electoral process in order to achieve his ends could hardly evoke anything but hostility among Saudi ruling circles, of course. No less a figure than King Fahd himself has declared that Islam and Saudi political history are "incompatible" with democracy.

In listening to and reading Sheikh Safar's comments on democracy one must keep well in mind that there are many sincere and convinced Muslim democrats. They find not only no contradiction in their commitments to both Islam and democracy but rather a necessary conjunction.

---

* See, for instance, the reference to "the ignorant, pagan, polytheistic society of the Arabian peninsula" in Safar al-Hawali's "In Defense of Woman."

The second point in political theory touched upon in the tapes occurs in no more than one sentence of Safar al-Hawali's lecture "The True Promise and the False One." In it, he firmly asserts that Muslims want to reestablish "the Caliphate." The statement is made in passing and Sheikh Safar makes no attempt to explain what he understands the term خلافة to mean.

Faraj Foda on the other hand was (until his assassination by Islamists for his heretical views) a self described "enlightened Muslim" who *has* examined the implications of the term "Caliphate." In his book الحقيقة الغائبة,* Foda -- like Fu'ad Zakariya and others -- accuses the Islamists of failing to define what their call for an Islamic state would entail. He notes that they are free with the claim that Muslims want to reinstate the Caliphate but asks what that might mean. He then proceeds to answer the question by reviewing, in both ideal and historical terms, what the Caliphate was.

In ideal terms Foda says the selection of a just ruler (خليفة ) arises from what amounts to a congress of notables (the اهل الربط و الحلّ --the people who bind and dissolve [bonds -- social commercial and political]); their "nomination" of a ruler is confirmed by the mass of the populace rendering the "oath of allegiance" ( البيعة). A pretty enough scenario in the ideal says Foda but one for which there is no historical basis and for the just application of which no institutions or procedures evolved at any point in Muslim history. In fact Muslim history is an unhappy succession of despots (rather than "just rulers") who have coerced their own nominations from the اهل الربط و الحلّ and the oath of allegiance from the populace. But, says Foda, even should a ruler be legitimately nominated and confirmed in office by the traditional ceremonies, what check would be placed on his absolute rule thereafter, and how would he be removed from office if unjust? Foda insists that these questions, never answered in Islamic history, are even more pressing today, and the Islamists have not even begun to address them. Unfortunately nowhere in the collection of tapes procured for this study have our Saudi Islamists proven him wrong.

---

* الحقيقة الغائبة (*The Missing Truth,*) Cairo: دار الفكر, 1986.

## Part 1

**"The Caliphate"** from ***The True Promise and the False One*** *by* **Safar al-Hawali.**

الدليل الاول الحرب العالمية الأولى . وقف فيها العرب مع من ؟ مع
الحلفاء ! ودخل العرب تحت الراية الانجليزية إلى بيت المقدس تحت
قيادة الجنرال الينبي الذي وضع ... ركز الرمح على جبل الزيتون وقال
<< الآن انتهت الحروب الصليبية >> والعرب جزء من جيشه . بعد ذلك
ماذا تم بعد نهاية الحرب العالمية الأولى؟ إتفاقية ساكس بيكو هي التي
طُبقت وأحلام العرب بأن الحلفاء سيعطونهم خلافة عربية لزعامة
الشريف حسين تبخرت وتقطعوا أو قطعوها إرباً قطعوا أوصال هذه
الامة حتى أن ولاية الشام وحدها قُسمت أربعة دول سورية ولبنان
وفلسطين والاردن وهي ولاية عثمانية واحدة كانت

The first indication [of Western hostility towards the Arabs] is the First World War. In it the Arabs stood with whom? With the Allies! The Arabs entered Jerusalem under the English flag under the command of General Allenby who placed ... set his standard on the Mount of Olives and said: "Now the Crusades are over, " while the Arabs were a part of his army! What happened after the end of the First World War? The "Sykes-Picot Agreement" is what was implemented, and the Arab dream that the Allies would give them an Arab Caliphate under the leadership of Sherif Hussien vanished. [The Arabs] were cut apart; or [the Europeans] divided [the Arab Caliphate] into pieces. They cut the bonds of this [Arab] nation such that even the Province of Syria itself was divided into four countries: Syria, Lebanon, Palestine, and Jordan when it had been only one Ottoman province.

## Part 2

### **"Democracy"** from ***The Meaning of Bin Baz's Statement*** by **Safar al-Hawali.**

#### Selection 1

موضوعُ الحدث الساعةَ كما يسمّى في الشرق والغرب هو موضوع
الجزائر . طبعاً نحن مبدئيا تعلمون الديمقراطية نعتقد أنها كفر .
هذا ما في عندنا فيه أي شك

The topic of conversation at this hour, as it is called in [both] the East and the West, is the matter of Algeria. Of course, we -- in principle ([as] you know) -- *democracy*, we believe that it is infidelity.* We do not have any doubt about this.

* Note the "topic-comment" sentence structure here which emphasizes "democracy" by placing it at the beginning of the clause.

#### Selection 2

نعتقد كذلك أن قيام الاسلام في الارض ليس بهذه الطرق وبهذه
الوسائل بالضرورة بل الطريق الصحيح والمنهج الحق هوالدعوة وطلب
العلم ونشر الفقه في الدين وتربية الناس على ذلك وحثهم على الامر
بالمعروف والنهي عن المنكر إلى أن تأتي مرحلة تمايز الصفوف إلى أن
يأتي الجهاد في سبيل الله وإقامة الدين بعد البيان والحجة وإبلاغ الحق
هذه يعني بديهيات معروفة والحمد لله

We also believe that establishing Islam on Earth is, of necessity, not [to be achieved] by these methods or through these means. Rather, the correct procedure, and the right system, is preaching, seeking knowledge, spreading religious knowledge, and educating people to that; encouraging them to "command the good and forbid evil"* until the stage of distinction in the ranks shall come; until the time of the *jihad*† for the sake of God and the implementation of religion shall come, after explanation, clarification and conveying the truth. These are, I mean, truisms--well-known, praise be to God.

* This is the fundamental Qur'anic injunction to Muslims; the phrase is found many time in the Qur'an.

† Jihad refers to the whole range of personal "struggle" against one's own sinfulness and wrong in the world "for the sake of God." The common translation as "Holy War" is profoundly misleading.

## Selection 3

لكن نحن نتكلم عن واقع عن قضية واقعة أمر واقع قد وقع لم يكن هناك مناص أو مفر من أحد أمرين : إما أن تقع أحداث كاحداث تونس هل تعلمون ما هي أحداث تونس ؟ في تونس الآن ما لا يقل عن خمسين ألف معتقل ومعتقلة ويعذبون بأشد أنواع التعذيب التي كانت في أيام جمال عبدالناصر نافذة على الجحيم وأمثالها كتبوا عن هذا . شئ فظيع وتواتر ونقله الثقات من الاخوة السلفين الموثقين في عقيدتهم ونقلهم والله وكتبوا ذلك وعندي أشياء كثيرة يعني مؤلمة مقلقة والله تُطيّر النوم تُذهب الراحة من القلوب ويعني ما أحب أن أنكد أو أنغّص عليكم بذكر التفاصيل المقصود كان يعني هذا احتمال هذا يعني حل لو تسيطرت الجبهة الخبيثة الاشتراكية الحاكمة أو جبهة الاخرى جبهة القوى الاشتراكية وهذا ما يريدون أن يفعلوا لابد من التنكيل والايذاء وضرب الصحوة والدعوة وفتح المعتقلات وهذا ما فعلوه في ايضا الجبهة واعضائها

But, we are talking about a certain reality, about an actual situation, an actual event which has happened. There was [sic] no escaping or evading one of two things: either that events like those in Tunisia should occur... do you know what the events in Tunisia are? There are, in Tunisia now, not less than fifty thousand male and female detainees. They are being tortured with the severest kinds of punishment which were, in the days of Gamal Abdul Nasser, "a Window into Hell" and others like them. [Former Tunisian detainees] have written about this. It is a scandalous thing. Trustworthy, *Salafi* * brothers, strong in their faith and their reporting, have gathered and transmitted [news of] it, by God. They have written it down. I have many things ... I mean they're painful and shocking, I swear to God, they rob you of your sleep. They disquiet your heart. I mean, I do not want to trouble and disturb you by talking about the details. My intention was, I mean, this is a possibility. This is a solution if the disgusting, ruling, socialist [National Liberation] Front wins or any other front, the front of socialist forces. This is what they want to do. There would be no escape from torture, punishment, striking down the [Islamic] Awakening and *da<sup>c</sup>wah*† , opening of detention centers. This is what they did to the [Islamic] party and its members [in Tunis].

* The term سَلَفِيّة [*salafiyyah*] is one often used by politically involved Muslims for their own movement, unlike most other commonly used terms which are applied to them by their adversaries. It derives from the term سَلَف [salaf] which refers to the earlierst generation of Muslims: "ancestors; forefathers." It suggests the need to return to the practices of their golden age.

† The *da<sup>c</sup>wah* or "call" (دَعْوَة) refers to Islamic proselytism or missionary work. Many individuals support "call" activities; both individuals and nations set up "Call Societies" to fund and support "missionary preachers" (داعٍ -الداعي /دُعاة) .

## Selection 4

البديل الاخر أنه على أن الديمقراطية كفر وعلى أن نتائج الانتخابات قد لا تكون مضمونة وعلى ما... ولكن تلافيا للتهم وأنكم غير شرعيين ندخل فيها ونرتكب أخف الضررين ونحقق أعلى المصلحتين ونثبت للغرب والشرق أن هذا الشعب لا يريد إلا الاسلام وهذه هو الذي عملت به الجبهة وكذلك في بعض الدول

The other alternative is -- despite the fact that democracy is infidelity and that the results of elections may not be guaranteed ... but to eliminate suspicions and [accusations which say:] "you [Muslim activists] are illegitimate we [should] enter [elections], commit the lesser of two evils, and achieve the greater of two goods. We will prove to the West and to the East that this people does not want anything but Islam. That is what the [Algerian Islamic Salvation] Front did; the same [has occurred] in some [other] nations.

## Selection 5

وهناك فتوى من سماحة الشيخ عبد العزيز بأنه إذا كانت الضرورة أو مصلحة الدعوة في دخول الانتخابات و البرلمان فلا بأس يعني طبعا بقيودها . هذا الذي فُعل على إية حال . تصوروا جبهة تحارب ويعتقل منها الالاف وإلى الان شيوخها في السجن الشيخ عباس مدني والشيخ على بلحاج في السجن ومع ذلك تأتي الانتخابات وتأتي هذه النتيجة العجيب

There is a *fatwa* * by His Eminence, Sheikh ᶜAbd al-ᶜAziz [Bin Baz] to the effect that if necessity or the good of the *da'wah* lies in entering elections and parliament -- then, there is no harm [in doing so]. I mean, of course, within the constraints [of the good of the *da'wah*]. This is what [the FIS] has done in any case. Imagine a Front struggling and thousands of [its members] being arrested. Until now its sheikhs in prison! Sheikh Abbas Madani, Sheikh Ali Belhajj, in prison! And, in spite of that, along come the elections, and along comes this astonishing result.

* A *fatwa* (فَتْوَى) is a written response to a question of law issued by a scholar of the law and stating the author's opinion on the issue. It is similar to a lawyer's "opinion" or a "friend of the court brief" in Anglo-American law; it is for the use of an individual or a court but is technically not binding on either (the question of its authority is complex, however).

## Selection 6

الحزب الحاكم ١٦ مقعد والجبهة ٢٠٢ وقد تزيد قد تصل الليلة إلى يمكن ٢١٠ صوت نسبة غريبة جداً تدل على أي شئ هذا الذي يفزع الغرب والشرق تدل على أن هذه الامة لا تريد ألا الاسلام

The Ruling Party: sixteen seats! The Front: 202! And, it might increase! Tonight, it might reach ... it might be 210 votes! An amazing percentage! What does this thing, which terrifies the West and the East, indicate? It indicates that this Community* does not want anything but Islam!

* The term أمّة ['ummah] is applied to the Muslim community as a whole regardless of other, especially national, identity. Hence an Arab Muslim and an Arab Christian may both be Egyptian (or Syrian, etc.) but only the Muslim is a member of the *'Ummah* while an Egyptian Muslim and an Indonesian Muslim have different languages, ethnicity and passports but are both members of the same "Community."

## Selection 7

لا نعني أنهم كلهم صحابة فضلاء علماء لا ليست كذلك لكن المقصود أن الرغبة العاطفة الشعور إسلامي يعني مستعد أن يتربى على الاسلام نعم في حاجة إلى تربية لكن جاي يقول لك أنا مستعد أن تربيني أوجد لي المنهج الاسلامي بدلا من المنهج الاشتراكي أوجد لي المحاضن الاسلامية بدل المحاضن الاشتراكية والعلمانية أوجد لي تعليم اللغة العربية بدل اللغة الفرنسية

We do not mean that they are all "Companions"* of the Prophet, eminent men, scholars. No! It's not that. But, what I mean is that the passionate desire, the Islamic feeling, is, I mean, ready to be trained in Islam. Yes, there is a need for education, but [the public] comes along saying: "I am ready for you to educate me. Give me Islamic curricula, instead of the socialist one; give me Islamic day-care centers, instead of socialist and secularist day-care centers; give me instruction in the Arabic language instead of the French language.

* The term "companions," of the Prohet Muhammad ( صَحابة رسول الله ), refers to the early circle of converts to Islam. They are especially venerated and the principle source for "traditions" (أحاديث) about the Prophet's sayings and deeds -- collectively his *Sunnah* ( سُنّة ). The Sunnah constitutes the second "source" (after the Qur'an) of Islamic law.

## Selection 8

علمني التفسير والتوحيد والفقه والحديث بدلا من تعليم المناهج الموجودة الآن من الكفر والالحاد والتاريخ القومي وغير ذلك المقصود هذه الدلالة يا إخوان دلالة أن الشعوب تريد الخير وشعب الجزائر ما شاء الله شعب غيور وصادق ومتدين بالفطرة والحمد لله

Teach me *Tafsir, Tawhid, Fiqh* and *Hadith** instead of the now existing systems of education in infidelity, atheism, national history and things like that. I mean, this sign, my brothers, is a sign that the people want the best; the Algerian people are, thank God, a zealous, honest, and religious people by nature, praise be to God.

* *Tafsir, Tawhid, Fiqh* and *Hadith* are respectively: "Qur'anic exegesis," "the concept and assertion of the absolute unity of the divine," "jurisprudential thought," and "Prophetic tradition" (the Sunnah -- the sayings and deeds of the Prophet.) Note that the terms are definite in Arabic, but referring (as they do) to the general concepts in question, they have intentionally been translated without any English article to express that generic sense.

## Selection 9

لما ظهر هذا الحدث الكبير تباينت ردود الفعل . فرنسا تلمّح بأن
الجيش يحل المشكلة . عجيب والله ! ليش الجيش ؟ أنتم دعاة
الديمقراطية تقولون فجر الديمقراطية في العالم الثورة الفرنسية لأنها
حررت الشعوب وعبرت عن إرادتها . طيب الشعب عبر عن إرادته .
لماذا تلمحون أن الحل لابد من تدخل الجيش ؟

When this great event occurred, reactions became apparent. France believes that the Army will solve the problem. Strange, by God! Why* the Army? You, democracy's preachers, say: "Democracy's dawn in the World [came with] the French Revolution because it liberated the people and expressed their will. OK, the [Algerian] people have expressed their will. Why do you intimate that the solution must involve intervention by the Army?

* Note the dialect interrogative here.

## Selection 10

بعض الدول والاذاعات والصحافة سكت ولم تتكلم مطلقا . ولا شئ !
ولو كانت جبهة اشتراكية في كلومبيا ولا في ثانية — جميكا ما
شسمها — دول ما أدري حتى فين تقع لجاء الخبر . ولكن في بلد
إسلامي كبير يعد حوالى ثلاثين مليون وأحداث خطيرة ولا شئ . بعض
الصحف كتبت وكتبت << جبهة الانقاذ >> ولم تذكر << الاسلامي . >>
ليش يعني << الانقاذ >> ؟ يعني هذا إنقاذ وهذه قوة وهذه تحرير كلها
زي بعض ! إسلامية ؟ لا سبحان الله لماذا لا تُذكر ؟

Some countries, the broadcast [media], the press kept quiet. They didn't speak up at all. Nothing! If it were a socialist front in Colombia or some second [country] -- Jamaica or whatever it's called -- some countries I don't even know where they might be, the news would come out. But in a big Muslim country with a population of about thirty million and serious events -- nothing! Some newspapers did write and wrote: "the Salvation Front," but they didn't mention "Islamic." I mean, why: "salvation"!? This is power; this is liberation, by God! It's all the same! "Islamic?" No! Glory be to God! Why was [Islam] not mentioned?

## Selection 11

بعض الصحف تجرأت أكثر ومنها جريدة الشرق الاوسط وقالت كلاما عجيبا هذه جريدة الشرق الاوسط نسأل الله العافية وانظروا حتى كلام الشيخ كيف يعني حاولت تحرفه وتؤول معناه وتثير البلبلة يعني بعناوين التي وضعتها من ذلك كلمة الشرق الاوسط عنوانها << كلمة لابد منها حول الانتخابات الجزائرية >> يقول إنّ ... قد علمتنا التجارب أن القوى التي تعيش في ظل قالب ايديلوجي — ايديلوجي معناها ايش؟ عقدي . يقول قالب عقدي جامد أو تتعرض للقهر والاضطهاد ولا تجد أمامها الفرصة الكافية للتنفيس أوالتعبير عن الرأي . تطرح شعارات مبسطة تتعاطف معها الجماهير

Some newspapers were more daring. Among them was *Al-Sharq al-Awsat*.* It said strange things, this *Sharaq al-Awsat* paper. We ask God to keep us well! See how, I mean -- even the Sheikh's† words, it tried to distort and misinterpreted their meaning to stir up confusion. I mean, by certain headlines which it set out. Among such things is a *Sharq Al-Awsat* commentary whose title is "A Word which Must be Said about the Algerian Elections." It says: "Experience has taught us that power which exists in an ideological form..." -- What does "ideological" mean? "Dogmatic." He says, "a dogmatic, rigid form" or "one subjected to pressure and oppression." You would not find, in it, sufficient chance to breathe or to express [your] opinion -- "... simple slogans are put out, and the masses sympathize with them."

* Saudi funded but independent daily headquartered in London.

† Sheikh Bin Baz, Saudi Arabia's highest ranking religious authority.

## Selection 12

افهموا يا عقلاء . شعارات مبسطة — الاسلام ولا كلام . والناس يتعاطفوا معه لانهم يصلون مغفلين . أكثر الناس مغفلين يصلوا ويصوموا ما هم مثقفين يعني هذا المقصود الذي يعني يريده العلمانين بهذه العبارات

Understand, O you thinking people! "Simple slogans" -- Islam! And, theology! And, "the people sympathize with it" because they, being simple-minded, pray; most of the people are simple-minded who pray and fast. They're not educated. I mean, this is the sense which the secularists want [to convey] by these phrases.

## Selection 13

بعدين تقول << ومع الوقت تصبح بعض الشعارات دغدغة أحلام بتذليل كل الصعاب وترياقا يعالج كل المشاكل . فيسهل تصديق هذه الشعارات وتتحول من زفرة للفت النظر إلى برنامج عمل سياسي. >>

Then [the editorial] says: "With time, some of these slogans become a stimulant to dreams of overcoming all difficulties; [the slogans become] an antidote which will treat all problems. It makes it easy to believe in these slogans. The[ slogans] turn from a groan [designed] to grab attention into a program for political action."

## Selection 14

كلام عن الجزائر من هي التي كسبت الجماهير من هي التي تحولت من زفرة أصبحت عمل سياسي سبحان الله الجبهة . انظروا كيف الطعن والدس وبعد ما يذكر قدوة يعني الاتحاد السوفيتي والدول الاشتراكية كما قارن أحمد جار الله الخبيث هذا وأمثاله النظام الشمولي عندهم يعنون الاسلام والشيوعية هذا نظام شمولي وهذا نظام شمولي يقول لك تجارب روسيا دلت على هذا وكذلك هنا تدل على ايش ؟ أن الحكم أكثر من مجرد شعارات ونية طيبة واستنهاض للهمم اوتحريض للشارع . ايش هي الحكم؟ المشاكل المتراكمة لا تحلها النظرات الميثالية ولا تنهض باعباء حلها الشعارات أو تغير الاسماء والوجوه وإنهاء سلطة هذا الحزب وإسناد الرأي على ذلك إنما تكمل الحلول في الرؤية الواقعية الإختبارية لحقيقة الاوضاع وفي العمل الصبور المدروس الصامت لكي تصبح الحرية والكساء والغذاء والطبابة في متناول كل عقل وكل جسد . يعني ابعدوا الدين

[How about] some talk about Algeria!? Who is it that has won the masses? Who is it that has changed from a groan [and] become political action? Glory be to God -- the Front! Look at the insult and the intrigue! And, after [the author of the editorial] has mentioned the Soviet Union and the Socialist countries as an example -- just as the loathsome Ahmad Jarullah and those like him have compared "their own" totalitarian system (they mean Islam) with communism (the former is a totalitarian system, and the latter is a totalitarian system) -- he says: "You have the Russian experience; it has shown this. And, here, likewise, what does [our situation] indicate? [Our situation] indicates that governance is more than mere slogans, good will, seeking to alleviate care, or rabble rousing. What is governance? Idealistic theories do not solve compounding problems nor can slogans, changing names and faces, ending one party's rule, or basing one's opinion on [such ideas as those] take up the burden of solving [ compounding problems]. Rather, solutions will be achieved through the realistic, experiential examination of the reality of circumstances and through patient, studied, silent work so that freedom, clothing, food and medical treatment come to be within the grasp of every mind and body." [That] means "banish religion."

Chapter Two

# Foreign Policy

## Introduction

One of the most prominent features of the 1992 "Memorandum of Advice" was its call for the abrogation of "all military commitments and treaties that encroach on the state's sovereignty and independence." The call came in clear response to the unsettling presence of American and European troops during, and in the wake of, the Gulf War, but how reminiscent it is of George Washington's warning against "entangling alliances." How reminiscent too of contemporary American conservatives' concerns about loss of U.S. sovereignty in the "new world order."

The Saudi Sheikhs agree that Saudi Arabia must no longer rely on "any external military force whatsoever to defend the country and protect its security." Sheikh Safar al-Hawali, in a three hour lecture entitled *The True Promise and the False One,** and Sheikh Salman al-'Awdah, in a "lesson" entitled *The Decisive Battle with Israel,* take up what might be categorized as the "foreign policy" issue. They expand upon the theme of the Memorandum of Advice's call for military self-sufficiency by explaining why it is utterly self-defeating to depend upon the West.

It is a commonplace of contemporary Muslim discourse to speak of the "new crusade" of a secular West seeking to impose its "hegemony" on the rest of the world. Muslims' fears are exacerbated by our politicians' eulogies of capitalism and "democracy," which are widely seen as precursors to the imposition of alien and destructive economic and political philosophies upon them. Those fears are only compounded by our hypocrisy in such cases as that of Algeria. The particular take on Western motivations, as expressed by Sheikh Safar especially, seems startling however.

---

* الوعد الحق والوعد المفترى lit. "The True Promise and the Forged Promise."

**"Christian Politics"** from ***The True Promise and the False One*** by **Safar al-Hawali.**

## Selection 1

القضية التي نريد أيها الإخوة الكرام أن نتحدث عنها في هذه الليلة ليست بعيدة ولا غريبة عن واقعنا اليومي فنحن كل يوم بل في كل نشرة أخبار وفي كل جريدة وفي كل لقاء يتم في هذه الأيام في وسائل الاعلام او في المجالس يكون الحديث عن هذا الحدث الكبير والقضية العظمى التي سنتناولها إن شاء الله تعالى بشئ من التفصيل الذي لابد منه إلا وهو ما يسمى مشروع السلام بين العرب واليهود.

The issue which we want, O you noble brothers, to talk about tonight is neither far from, nor strange to, our daily reality. We, each day (or rather in every news report and in every newspaper and in every casual meeting which takes place these days -- in the information media or in get-togethers), the talk is about this great event and the momentous issue which we will treat, God -- may He be exalted -- willing, in some detail, from which (detail) there is no escape in as much as it is what is being called the peace process between the Arabs and the Jews.

## Selection 2

ولا شك أن ما جرى في مدريد أيها الإخوة الكرام لا شك أنه حدث تاريخي كبير جداً ولا أدل على ذلك من اشتغال وسائل الإعلام الغربية بالذات ثم العالمية الأخرى من اشتغالها بهذا الحدث تحليلاً وتعليقا حتى أن الغرب تناسى مشاكله الداخلية وقضاياه الكبرى واشتغل قادته ومفكروه وصحافيوه ومراسلوه وافراد شعبه كلهم بهذه القضية وملاحقة هذا الحدث لحظة بلحظة وساعة بساعة

And, there is no doubt that what has happened in Madrid, O you noble brothers, there is no doubt that it is a very great historical event. And, nothing is more suggestive of that than the preoccupation of the Western news media, in particular, and then the international [news media] because of their preoccupation with this incident, with its analysis and commentary till the West even seems to have forgotten its internal problems and its greatest issues. And, its leaders, intellectuals, journalists, reporters and bureaucrats, all of them, have become preoccupied, following this event moment by moment and hour by hour.

## Selection 3

فما السر في ذلك أيها الاخوة الكرام؟ هل تتوقعون أن يكون سببَ ذلك ... أو أن يكون سببُ ذلك هو أن طرفين كانا متنازعين فأصلح بينهما أو يراد أن يُصلح بينهما؟ لا . إن ما تم في مدريد أيها الإخوة الكرام يفوق ذلك بمراحل كثيرة . إن مدريد في الحقيقة هي محطة لقطار طويل انطلق منذ ألفي سنة وإن شئتم وكما سنُثبت فنقول إنه انطلق منذ خمسة آلاف سنة وسيستمر إلى أن تقوم الساعة وهذه مدريد ومن بعدها واشنطن محطات عابرة على هذا الطريق الطويل وهذا الطريق الطويل هو طريق الوعد الذي وعد الله تبارك وتعالى به نبيه وخليله ابراهيم عليه السلام ووعد به صالح ذريته من بعده هذا الوعد أيها الإخوة الكرام تلتقي عنده الاديان الثلاثة المعروفة في العالم كلها

So, what is the secret of that, O honorable brothers? Would you expect that the reason for this ... or that the *reason* for this* is that two parties were having a dispute and that peace had been made between them? Or, that it was intended to make peace between the two? No! What has happened in Madrid, O honorable brothers, goes beyond that by many stages. Madrid, in truth, is a way station for a long train which set out two thousand years ago, or if you wish -- and as we will prove, we can say that it set out five thousand years ago and will continue until the "Hour" [of Judgement] arrives. This Madrid, and after it Washington, are passing stations on this long road. This long road is the way of the promise which God, may He be praised and exalted, made to His prophet and friend Ibrahim (peace be upon him) and made to the virtuous among [Ibrahim's] descendants after him. This promise, O honorable brothers, the three religions well known to the world come together over it.

* Notice that this repetition arises as the speaker corrects his use of the case system, changing the incorrect accusative in the first instance to the proper nominative in the second.

## Selection 4

المسلمون لهم في هذا الوعد دعوى ولكنها ثابتة ولله الحمد في كتاب الله وبسنة رسول الله صلى الله عليه وسلم كما سنبين واليهود والنصارى لهم نظرة إلى هذا الوعد الذي افتروه على الله تبارك وتعالى ومن ثمّ فإن الصراع في الحقيقة ليس بين قوميتين ولا بين دول وإنما هو صراع بين وعدين بين الوعد الحق وبين الوعد المفترى . وبالتالي فهو صراع بين عقيدتين بين عقيدة التوحيد التي جاء بها ابراهيم عليه السلام ثم جددها محمد صلى الله عليه وسلم وسيجددها عيسى ابن مريم عليه السلام في آخر الزمان وبين دعوة الشرك والخرافة والدجل التي أسسها الأحبار والرهبان فيما كتبوه من عند انفسهم وقالوا هذا من عند الله وما هو من عند الله ابتداءً بحاخامات اليهود ومروراً ببولس -- شاؤول — ثم البابوات الضالون المضلون ثم انتهاءً بهرتزل ومن كان معه ثم ينتهي الامر — النهاية المؤكدة — في آخر الزمان بظهور مسيحهم الدجال وعندما يلتقي المسيحان — المسيح ابن مريم عليه السلام والمسيح الدجال — عندئذ تنتهي هذه المعركة الطويلة الابدية بين هذين الوعدين أي بين الامتين اللتين تؤمنان بهذا الوعد أمة الاسلام من جهة واليهود والنصارى — أهل الكتاب — من جهة أخرى

Muslims have a claim to this promise, and it is confirmed, praise be to God, in God's Book and in the Sunnah of the Prophet of God, may God bless him and grant him peace, as we will make clear. The Jews and Christians have a [different] point of view on this Promise which they falsely ascribed to God, may He be glorified and exalted. Therefore, the conflict, in fact, is not between two nationalisms nor is it between states. Rather, it is a conflict between two promises, the true promise and the false one. Furthermore, it is a conflict between two doctrines; between the doctrine of *Tawhid* which Ibrahim, may peace be upon him, brought forth and which was then renewed by Muhammad, may God bless him and grant him peace, and which Jesus the son of Mary will renew at the end of time, and between the claim of polytheism, superstition and deceit which the rabbis and monks founded through that which they, themselves, wrote. They said, "This is from God," but it is not from God. Beginning with the Jewish rabbis and moving on to Paul-- Saul, and then the Popes, going astray and leading astray, then finally Herzl and those who were with him. Then, the matter will finally have a definite outcome with the appearance of their anti-Christ. When the two Messiahs -- Jesus the Son of Mary and their anti-Christ -- meet, at that moment, this long, eternal battle between these two promises, that is between the two nations that believe in this promise -- the nation of Islam on the one hand and the Jews and Christians -- the people of the Book -- on the other hand, will end.

## Selection 5

هذه هي القضية المهمة أيها الإخوة . ولذلك فإن ما جرى أو يجري وما قُرر في مدريد ليس في حقيقته بيانات أو قرارات للصلح وإنما هو للمتأمل المتدبر — وكما سنُثبت بالادلة والبراهين القاطعة إن شاء الله — إنما هو تأييد وإيمان بالوعد المفترى وتكذيب وكفر بالوعد الحق. وهذه هي جوهر القضية . وهذا هو أساسها . ولا يشغلنا بعد ذلك الحديث في تفصيلات — ماذا جرى وماذا سيجري وما هي النتائج وإن كنا سنتعرض لها إن شاء الله . لكن القضية — الاساس — هي هذه القضية والتي سنبدأ إن شاء الله تعالى الحديث عنها مع طوله كما ذكرنا

That is the important issue, O brothers. Therefore, what has happened, or is happening and what has been resolved, in Madrid is not, in fact, statements or resolutions on peace. Rather, it is, for the thoughtful observer -- as we will prove with decisive evidences and proofs (God willing), a mere support of and belief in the false promise, a falsification of and disbelief in the true promise. This is the core of the issue; this is its foundation. Thereafter, talk about the details of what has happened or what is going to happen and what the results will be need not occupy us (even should we be exposed to it) God willing. However, the issue, the basis, is this matter which we will begin -- God willing -- to talk about at length as we mentioned earlier.

## Selection 6

فـالله تبـارك وتـعـالى كمـا يزعـمـون قـد وعـد ابراهيم عليـه السـلام في
التوراة وسنقرأ لكم نص التوراة في الوعود التي يستند اليها اليهود.
وأمـا الوعـد الحق الذي وعـد الله تبـارك وتعـالى بـه أوليـاءه فـمـعـروف
لدى الجـمـيع وقـد قـرأه الامـام ... في الصـلاه قـرأ بـعـض أدلتـه و
سنعود له في الاخير إن شاءالله تبارك وتعالى

Now, God (may He be glorified and exalted) --as they claim-- made a promise to Abraham, may peace be upon him, in the Torah. We'll read to you the text of the Torah concerning the promise upon which the Jews base [their claims]. But as for the true promise which God (may He be glorified and exalted) made to his [Muslim] "saints," it is well known to all. The Imam recited ... during the prayer he recited some of the evidences for [ the true promise], and we will return to it, at the end, if God (may He be glorified and exalted) so wills.

## Selection 7

تبدأ القصة العجيبة في عهد نوح عليه السلام . نبتدئ بعهد نوح عليه
السلام لأنه المفتاح لفهم ما سيجري من وعد لابراهيم عليهما السلام .
تقول التوراة المحرّفة « وابتدأ نوح يكون فلاحاً وغرس كرماً وشرب
من الخمر . » والعياذ بالله . هذا ... كلكم تقشعر جلودكم أن يوصف
الأنبياء بهذا لكن هذا منطوق التوراة وهذا لفظها وستعلمون لماذا
افتعلوا هذه التهمة الشنيعة . قالوا « وشرب من الخمر فسكر وتعرى
داخل خبائه فأبصر حام ابو كنعان عورة ابيه وأخبر أخويه خارجا . »
« حام ابن نوح ابو كنعان» ... هكذا عرفوه « ابو كنعان » رأى
عورة ابيه كما يزعمون فخرج إلى اخويه وقال لهم « إن ابي هكذا .»
قال « فأخذ سام ويافث الرداء وضعاه على أكتافهما ومشيا الى الوراء
وسترا عورة ابيهما ووجهاهما إلى الوراء فلم يُبصرا عورة ابيهما»
هذا الآن من هنا تنقسم البشرية إلى قسمين كما ترون . « فلما
استيقظ نوح من خمره ( كما يقولون ) علم ما فعل به ابنه الصغير
فقال ملعون!...» مين ؟ كنعان . طيب — ايش ذنب كنعان ؟ ما وُلد
الا الان كنعان ! « ملعون كنعان .» « عبد العبيد يكون لإخوته » —
« عبد العبيد يكون لإخوته! » وقال « مبارك الرب إله سام» بارك

سام ولعن كنعان قال «وليكن كنعان عبداً لهم ليفتح الله ليافث فيسكن في مساكن سام وليكن كنعان عبداِ لهم» ثلاث مرات التأكيد بأن كنعان يكون عبداً للجنسين الأخرين . مَن هو كنعان؟ العرب.

The astonishing story starts in the time of Noah, may peace be upon him. We begin with the time of Noah because it is the key to understanding what is going to happen after a promise to Abraham, may peace be upon both of them. The corrupted Torah says : " Noah started out being a farmer. He planted a vineyard and drank some of the wine." [All] protection [from sin] is in God! This ... the skin of each and every one of you crawls when the Prophets are described like this, but this is the Torah's text. This is its wording, and you will come to know why they fabricated this horrible accusation. They said, "He drank some of the wine, got drunk and lay naked inside his tent. Then Ham, the father of Canaan, saw his father naked and told his two brothers outside." Ham, the son of Noah is "the father of Canaan." This is how they identified [Ham] -- the father of Canaan. [Ham] saw his father's nakedness -- so they assert -- and went out to his brothers and said "my father is such and such." [The text] says, "So Shem and Yapheth took a cloak, put it on their shoulders, walked backwards and covered their father's nakedness their faces turned backwards, so they did not see their father's nakedness." This now ... it's from here that the human race will be divided into two groups, as you will see. "So, when Noah awoke from his wine," as they say, "he learned what his younger son had done to him, and he said...." Cursed be who? Canaan! But what was Canaan's sin?! He was not yet even born! "A slave of slaves shall he be to his brothers!" A slave of slaves to his brothers. [The text] said, "Blessed be the Lord, the God of Shem." He blessed Shem and cursed Canaan. [The text] said, "Let Canaan be a slave to them so that God might make things easy for Yapheth. So he shall live in Shem's dwellings and let Canaan be a slave to them." Three times the confirmation that Canaan would be a slave for the other two races. Now, who is Canaan? The Arabs.

## Selection 8

هذا من أول ما يبدأ الانسان يا إخوان يقرأ التوراة يقرأه . وهذا الكلام تقرأه المدارس الانجيلية في الولايات المتحدة الامريكية من أول ما يدخل الطالب السنة الاولى الابتدائية وعدد هذه المدارس لا يقل عن عشرين ألف مدرسة يدرس بها ملايين التلاميذ كما سنبين إن شاء الله تعالى

This is the first thing a person, O brothers, would read when he begins to read the Torah. This language, Christian schools in the United States of America read it as soon as the student enters first grade elementary. The number of those schools is not less than twenty thousand, in which millions of students study as we will show, God (may He be exalted) willing.

## Selection 9

في الاصحاح الخامس عشر يحدد ... تحدد التوراة المحرفة الارض التي هي ملك وحق أبدي . فتقول << لنسلك أعطي هذه الارض من نهر مصر إلى النهر الكبير >> — نهر الفرات . ثم بعد ذلك يقول << يستعبد لك شعوب وتسجد لك قبائل كن سيداً ( هذا ليعقوب) لإخوتك وليسجد لك بنوا أمك ليكن لاعنوك ملعونين ومباركوك مباركين>>

In chapter fifteen,* the corrupted Torah defines ... defines the land which is the property and eternal right (of the Jews). It says: "To your offspring I give this land from the Egyptian river to the great river" -- the Euphrates River. Then after that, it says: "Nations will be enslaved to you and tribes will bow down before you. Be master (this is to Jacob) to your brothers, and have the sons of your mother bow down before you. May the ones who curse you be cursed and the ones that bless you be blessed."†

* Genesis 15:18.

† Genesis 27:29.

## Selection 10

هنا يأتي إشكال . ولابد أنه يثور عند كثير من الأخوة . فيقال إذا كان هذا ما يؤمن به اليهود ويعتقدونه فيحق لهم باعتبارهم يهوداً لكن ما دخل النصارى ؟ المتوقع أن يكون النصارى مع من؟ مع المسلمين لأن الذين — بزعم النصارى — قتلوا المسيح ( وما قتلوه وما صلبوه كما نعتقد لكن بزعمهم هم ) الذين قتلوا نبيهم وآذووا الحواريين واضطهدوهم وفعلوا ما فعلوا بالمسيحيين الأوائل بالنصارى الأوائل هم من ؟ هم اليهود .

A problem comes up here. Of course many of [our] brothers will be furious, but it [could be] said: "If this is what the Jews believe and hold, that's their right in consideration of [the fact that] they are Jews, but what have the Christians to do with it? With whom should the Christians be expected to side? With the Muslims! Because, the ones who, according to the Christians' assertion, killed the Messiah -- they didn't kill him, and they didn't crucify him as far as we believe* -- but by [the Christians'] own assertion, the ones who killed their prophet and hurt and oppressed his disciples and who did what they did to early Christians, to the early Nazarenes-- who were they? The Jews!

* Qur'an 4:157.

## Selection 11

وعيسى عليه السلام في آخر الزمان سينزل ونحن نتفق معهم في هذا أما اليهود يعتقدون أن عيسى عليه السلام نبي دجال كذاب ولن يعود مرة أخرى . إذاً سبحان الله أي الطائفتين أقرب؟ كان المفروض أن يكون النصارى معنا ضد اليهود ولكن لا سبحان الله استطاع اليهود بمكرهم وخبثهم ودهائهم وبغباوة النصارى وانسياقهم وراء اليهود أن يقلبوا ذلك رأساً على عقب

And Jesus, peace be upon him, will, at the end of time, come down, and we agree with them on this. But, the Jews believe that Jesus, peace be upon him, is a false prophet and a liar. He will not come back another time. So, may God be glorified, which of the two groups is closer? It ought to have been that the

Christians were with us against the Jews, but no! May God be glorified. The Jews were able -- by their deception, wickedness and cunning and because of the Christians' stupidity and blind following of the Jews -- to turn matters head over heels.

### Selection 12

استغلوا ماذا؟ استغلوا أن الكتاب الذي يؤمن به اليهود والنصارى معاً الكتاب المقدس كما يسمونه يتكون من عهدين أو من قسمين القسم الاول العهد ايش؟ القديم والثاني العهد الجديد. العهد القديم هو التوراة بما فيها هذا الكلام الذي قرأناه فأي نصراني يبتدئ يقرأ كتابه أول ما يقرأ مثل هذا الكلام وأضعاف كثيرة مثله إذاً فهم يؤمنون بما يؤمن به اليهود نتيجة لهذا. هذه يعني أحد الاسباب والسبب الآخر كما تعلمون جميعاً ما جُبل عليه أهل الكتاب مما بينه الله تبارك وتعالى في مواضع كثيرة من كتابه من الحسد لهذه الامة. فالنصارى حسدوا هذه الامة رغم معرفتهم كما قد آمن النجاشي وكما قد كاد أن يؤمن هرقل وغيرهم كثير رغم المعرفة المؤكدة برسول الله صلى الله عليه وسلم وصدق رسالته.

What did they exploit? They exploited [the fact that] the book in which the Jews and the Christians both believe -- the "Sacred Book" as they call it -- consists of two "testaments" or of two parts. The first part is which testament? The "Old [Testament]" and the second is the "New Testament."* The Old Testament is the Torah which includes this discourse that we have [just] read. So any Christian who begins reading his Book, the first thing he reads is this kind of discourse, and many times its like. So, [the Christians] believe in what the Jews believe as a result of that. This, I mean, is one of the reasons. The other reason, as you all know, is the envy to which the People of the Book are inclined at that [benificence] which God, may He be blessed and exalted, has shown, in many places in His Book, to this [Islamic] community. The Christians have envied this community despite their knowing that the Negus believed in [Islam] and that Heraclius was also on the point of believing [as were] many others -- despite their certain knowledge of the Prophet of God, may God bless him and grant him peace, and the truth of his message.

* Note the audience response here.

## Selection 13

هناك قضية مهمة جداً في سياق التاريخ المعاصر لأننا سنضطر أن ننتقل إلى التاريخ المعاصر لكن نريد أن نقدم بهذا الأمر المهم . وهي أنه الغرب يكون أشد عداوة لنا في المرحلة التي نكون نحن أشد تعلقاً فيها به هذه قضية لاحظوا كيف . يكون الغرب أشد عداوة لنا أهل الكتاب يكونون أشد عداوة لنا في الوقت الذي نكون نحن فيه أشد تعلقاً بهم وتمسكاً بهم وتحالفاً معهم

There is a very important issue in the context of contemporary history because we will be compelled to turn to contemporary history. But, we want to introduce [it] with this important matter. It is that the West has the greatest animosity toward us at the very stage during which we are most linked to them. That is a problem. Notice how [this works]. The West is most hostile to us, the People of the Book are most hostile to us, at the very time during which we are most linked to them, most clinging to them, most allied with them.

## Selection 14

الدليل الاول الحرب العالمية الأولى وقف فيها العرب مع من ؟ مع الحلفاء ودخل العرب تحت الراية الانجليزية إلى بيت المقدس تحت قيادة الجنرال الينبي الذي وضع ... ركز الرمح على جبل الزيتون وقال الآن انتهت الحروب الصليبية والعرب جزء من جيشه . بعد ذلك ماذا تم بعد نهاية الحرب العالمية الأولى؟ اتفاقية ساكس بيكو هي التي طبقت وأحلام العرب بأن الحلفاء سيعطونهم خلافة عربية بزعامة الشريف حسين تبخرت وتقطعوا أو قطعوها إرباً. قطعوا أوصال هذه الامة حتى أن ولاية الشام وحدها قسمت أربعة دول سورية ولبنان وفلسطين والاردن وهي ولاية عثمانية واحدة كانت

The first indication [of Western hostility] is the First World War. In it, the Arabs stood with whom? With the Allies. The Arabs entered, under the English flag, Jerusalem -- under the command of General Allenby who placed, set up, [his] standard on the Mount of Olives and said: "Now the Crusader wars are over" while the Arabs were a part of his army! After that ... what happened after the end of the First World War? The "Sykes-Picot Agreement" was what was implemented, and the Arabs' dreams that the Allies would give them an Arab Caliphate under the leadership of the Sherif Hussien went up in smoke. [The Arabs] were divided, or [the Europeans] divided [the Caliphate] into pieces. They cut the bonds of the community so far that even the Province of Syria alone was divided into four states: Syria, Lebanon, Palestine and Jordan while it had been one Ottoman province.

## Selection 15

والقضية الأخرى والشاهد الآخر عندما قامت الحرب العالمية الثانية وكانت بريطانية تحتل أكثر بلاد العالم الاسلامي هي وفرنسا أخذوا يجندون الجنود من الهند ومن غيرها بالنسبة للانجليز وكذلك من شمال افريقيا بالنسبة للفرنسيين ويأتون بالمشايخ السوء والمفتين ويقولون لهم افتوا المسلمين بأن قتال الالمان جهاد في سبيل الله

The other issue and the other evidence -- when World War II broke out and Britain was in occupation of most of the countries of the Muslim world, it and France, they began recruiting soldiers from India and elsewhere with regard to the British and similarly from North Africa with regard to the French. They would bring out evil Sheikhs and Muftis and say to them: "Advise Muslims that fighting the Germans is Jihad in the path of God.

## Selection 16

فماذا حصل بعد انتهاء الحرب العالمية ؟ الذي حصل هو قيام دولة إسرائيل وتحقيق وعد بلفور. في الحرب العالمية الاولى كانت القضية تحت ستار عصبة الامم ونقاط الرئيس ولسن . في الحرب العالمية الثانية كانت القضية مغلفة بميثاق الامم المتحدة وحقوق الانسان التي في تلك السنة التي أنشئت فيها دولة إسرائيل أعلنت حقوق الانسان حتى نعرف حقوق من من البشر يريدون هذه حربين

Then, what happened after the World War? The thing that happened is the establishment of the state of Israel and the implementation of the Balfour Declaration. In the First World War, the issue was under the cover of the League of Nations and President Wilson' s ["Four] Points." In Second World War, the issue was covered by the Charter of the United Nations and "Human Rights" which, in that [very] year in which the state of Israel was founded, "Human Rights" were declared so we would understand which part of humanity's rights they were talking about. These are two wars.

## Selection 17

الحرب الثالثة كانت حرب الخليج وكلكم يعلم ماذا جرى فيها وماذا دار و في النهاية ما يزال العرب متعلقين متمسكين بالغرب وواثقين في وعوده وسوف يرون وسوف نرى جميعاً بأم عيننا ماذا سيفعل الغرب بنا كما فعل بنا في المرات السابقة

The third war was the Gulf War, and you all know what happened and what turned out during it. And, in the end, the Arabs are still linked to and holding with the West and are [still] trusting its promises. And, they will see (as we all shall see with our own eyes) what the West will do with us, as it did with us in previous times.

## Selection 18

نركز الحديث الآن عن النصارى لأننا كما قلت مخدوعون بهم ومغرر بنا من كلامهم ونعطيهم الثقة الكاملة مع أنهم سيفعلون بنا ما سنراه بأم أعيننا ولاحول ولا قوة الا بالله . هناك عقيدة عند النصارى تقول إن المسيح سيرجع بعد ألف سنة . في أول ما ... يعني بعد أن رُفع عليه السلام قالوا سيرجع المسيح بعد ألف سنة ثم يحكم العالم ألف سنة ولهذا عندما كان عام ألف ميلادية يعني قبل كم؟ قبل حوالى ألف سنة من الآن انتظر النصارى في جميع انحاء العالم مجئ المسيح وانتظروا وانتظروا ما جاء فهدأ الموضوع لما جاء هذا القرن الآن قارب على الانتهاء بدأت الدعوات تظهر في جميع أنحاء العالم النصراني بأن المسيح في عام ألفين سيعود طيب وكيف يعود؟ قالوا إذا عاد المسيح فإنه سيعود في مملكة إسرائيل في فلسطين في موطنه الاصلي ولذلك يرى النصارى أن تجميع اليهود في أرض فلسطين هو مقدمة لقدوم المسيح ولعودة المسيح الألفية ومن هنا تبنى النصارى منذ أربعة قرون وليس اليهود ... النصارى قبل اليهود تبنى القضية تجميع بني إسرائيل في أرض فلسطين تمهيداً لعودة المسيح في الالف سنة الثالثة

# Chapter Two

We will now focus [our] discussion on the Christians because we, as I said, are deluded by them, and we are fooled by their discourse. We place complete confidence [in] them even though they will do with us what we shall see with our own eyes -- there is no power and no strength save in God! There is a belief among the Christians which says: "The Messiah will return after a thousand years." As soon as ... I mean, after he was raised up -- may peace be upon him, they said: "the Messiah will return after a thousand years; then he will rule the world for a thousand years." Because of that, when it was the year one thousand *anno domine* -- that means how long ago? About a thousand years ago, from now -- the Christians in all parts of the world were waiting for the "[Second] Coming" of the Messiah. They waited and waited, but he didn't come. So, the subject fell quiet. [Then] when this century was coming, now, close to [its] end, preachings began to appear in all parts of the Christian world [to the effect] that the Messiah would return in the year two thousand. Fine! And, how would he return? They said: "When the Messiah returns, he will return in the "Kingdom of Israel" in Palestine in his original homeland. Therefore, the Christians believe that the gathering of Jews in Palestine is a precursor of the coming of the Messiah and the Millennial return of the Messiah. And, from this point the Christians adopted, four centuries ago -- and not the Jews ... the Christians before the Jews -- adopted the issue -- gathering the Jews in Palestine as a preparation for the return of the Messiah in the third millennium.

## Selection 19

ظهر كتاب في أمريكا ألفه رجل يدعى اوترال روبرتس وهذا كتاب مشهور جداً سماه درامة نهاية الزمن وكتاب آخر أكثر منه شهرة وهو كتاب الذي ألفه لندسي كتاب نهاية أعظم كرة أرضية هذا الكتاب أو هذان الكتابان كمثالين يفترضان أن عام ألفين أو قريباً منه سوف تنتهى هذه الكرة الارضية نهائيا

A book has appeared in America that a man called Oral Roberts wrote. This is a very famous book; he called it *The Drama of the End of the World*. Another book, even more famous than it -- it being a book which "Lindsey" wrote, is the book *The Last Days of the Late Great Planet Earth.* This book, or these two books -- as examples, suppose that [by] the year two thousand, or close to it, this earthly sphere will come to a final end.

## Selection 20

كيف تنتهي ؟ قالوا كل الحضارات تنتهي حتى كان واحد منهم يقول لا داعي أن تفكروا في ديون أمريكا الخارجية ولا داعي تفكروا في مستقبل أجيال من بعد ولا تفكروا في ارتفاع الضرائب في أمريكا العملية هي بضعة سنوات وتنتهي كيف تنتهي؟ قالوا ستقوم المعركة الكبرى العالمية معركة هرمجدون أو سهل مجدو وهذه المعركة ستكون بين الوثنيين وبين النصارى ولابد أنكم سمعتم عن هذه المعركة كثيراً قبل حرب الخليج وكيف أن الرأى العام في أمريكا حُشد حشداً قوياً للتصديق بأن الحرب هي حرب هرمجدون أو سهل مجدو سهل مجدو هذا سهل صغير في فلسطين يقولون إن المعركة العالمية النهائية ستكون فيه بين جيوش يصل عددها إلى أربعمائة مليون مع أنه لا يمكن أن الارض تحتمل بهذا العدد

How is it going to end? They have said: "All civilizations end." One of them even said: "There's no call for you to think about America's foreign debts, and there is no call to think about the future of the next generations. Do not think about rising taxes in America. The issue is [a matter] of a few years, and it will [all] end." How is it going to end? They have said: "The [final] great world struggle will happen" -- the battle of Armageddon or Mageddo Plain. This battle will be between the pagans and the Christians. You must have heard much about this battle before the Gulf War and how public opinion in America was strongly prepared to believe that this war was the battle of Armageddon or Mageddo Plain. This Mageddo Plain is a small plain in Palestine; they say that the final world battle will take place in it between armies whose number will reach four hundred million even though the territory could not hold such a number.

## Selection 21

لكن يقولون في هذه الايام وقريب من عام ألفين ستكون هذه المعركة وستكون حرباً نووية ستكون الحرب نووية وسوف يأتي المسيح فيرفع المؤمنين به فوق السحاب ويموت المشركون الوثنيون يعني بعض الكلام هذا بعض الاخوان يقول سبحان الله هذا الكلام يصدقونه الامريكان ؟! عندنا أكثر من دليل أكثر من إحدى عشر مرة يعلن

الرئيس ريغان إيمانه بهذا رئيس الولايات المتحدة وبوش وغيره
لعلنا نأتي بكثير من الشواهد فضلا عن الطبقة المثقفة فضلا عن كثير
من ... طبعاً كل رجال الدين يؤمنون بهذه القضية وأن المعركة لابد
منها قد يختلفون في التاريخ لكن لابد من المعركة هذه والوثنيون
الذين سيقتلون هم الكنعانيون

But, they say: "In these days, close to the year two thousand, this battle will occur, and it will be a nuclear war." The war will be nuclear! The Messiah will come, and he will lift those who believe in him above the clouds while the polytheist pagans will die. I mean, some of this talk...! Our brothers say: " Glory be to God!" This talk! The Americans believe it?! We have more than one proof [of that]. More than eleven times, President Reagan has announced his belief in this [proposition], the president of the United States! And Bush and others! Maybe we should bring out more proofs ... except for the educated class and except for many of .... Of course, all men of religion believe in this matter, and [they believe] that the battle must be. They may differ on the date but this battle must happen. And, the pagans who will be killed ...? They are the Canaanites.

## Selection 22

الرئيس نكسون وهو أكبر رؤساء أمريكا تنظيراً وفكراً ألف كتاباً
يعني يشعركم بهذه القضية عنوانه ١٩٩٩ نصر بلا حرب يقول << إلى
عام ١٩٩٩ نكون قد حققنا السيادة الكاملة على العالم من غير حرب >>
يعني بالنسبة لامريكا كدولة << بعد ذلك يبقى ما بقي على المسيح >>
لا يتدخلون هم فيه يعني هم يحددون ... لا يأتي عام الفين إلا وقد
هيأوا لعودته وما بقي عليه وكما يقولون هذا الكلام الذي يعتقده
الرئيس نكسون ... لعلنا نقرأ بعض مقاطع صغيرة من كتابه هذا
الضخم يقول نكسون أولاً << عندما جوربتشوف زار واشنطون... >>
(وهذه من ثمرات النفاق هذه العداء من ثمرات النفاق بين الشرق
والغرب هذا الحرب الشرسة على الاسلام) يقول نكسون << يجب على
روسيا وأمريكا أن تعقدا تعاوناً حاسماً لضرب الاصولية الاسلامية >>

President Nixon, he being the most observant and thoughtful of the [recent] presidents, wrote a book -- I mean it will give you a sense of this matter -- whose title is *1999: Victory without War*. He says: "By the year 1999, we will have gained complete leadership of the world without war." He means as regards America as a state. "After that, [only] that which is to be left to the Messiah will remain [to be done]." They, themselves, will not interfere in it. This means, they will determine .... the year 2000 will not come [before] they have gotten ready for [the Messiahs's] return and that which remains for Him [to do], as they say. This is the discourse which President Nixon believes! Perhaps we might read in some small parts of this large book of his. Nixon says, first: "When Gorbachev visited Washington...." (And, these are some of the fruits of hypocrisy; this animosity is some of the fruit of the hypocrisy between the East and the West -- the fierce war on Islam) ... Nixon says: "Russia and America must establish a decisive cooperation to strike at Islamic fundamentalism."

## Selection 23

يقول نكسون << إن صراع العرب ضد اليهود يتطور (هذا الصراع الموجود الآن يتطور) الى نزاع بين الأصوليين الاسلاميين من جانب وإسرائيل والدول العربية المعتدلة من جانب آخر >> هذه هي المعركة << المعركة ليست تقوم بيننا وبين العرب المعتدلين >> وكرر هذا وفصله ولكن خلاصة الموضوع كما قال<< المعركة ستكون بين الأصوليين الاسلاميين من جانب وبين إسرائيل وأمريكا والعرب المعتدلين من جانب آخر>>

Nixon says: "The conflict of the Arabs against the Jews will develop. This now present conflict will develop into a dispute between Muslim fundamentalists on the one side and the Jews and the moderate Arab states on the other." This is the battle. "The battle will not break out between us and the moderate Arabs." He repeated this and described it in detail, but a summation of the subject is, as he said, "The battle will be between the Muslim fundamentalists on the one side and Israel and America and the moderate Arabs on the other side."

## Selection 24

هذه حقيقة المعركة ويقول << في العالم الاسلامي من المغرب إلى إندونيسيا ورثت الآصولية الاسلامية محل الشيوعية باعتبارها الاداة الاساسية للتغير العنيف >> يعني العنف والارهاب الذي كنا أول نقول نطلقه على الشيوعية انتهى الآن ورثته الصحوة الاسلامية من

المغرب إلى إندونيسيا لاحظتوا كيف ؟ ويختم كتابه بعبارات
حماسية عجيبة نذكر واحدة منها يقول « عندما كانت أمريكا ضعيفة
وفقيرة منذ مائتي سنة مضت كانت عقيدتنا هي المبقية علينا»
لاحظوا «وعلى ... و نحن ... وعلينا ونحن ندخل قرننا الثالث »
بالنسبة لعمر أمريكا « و نستقبل الألف السنة المقبلة أن نعيد
اكتشاف عقيدتنا ونبث فيها الحيوية » إذاً حتى الرئيس نكسون
يؤمن بالأصولية المتطرفة طبعاً ما يسمى متطرفاً لأنه ليس داعياً
إسلامياً

This is the reality of the battle. He says: "In the Muslim world, from Morocco to Indonesia, Muslim fundamentalism has inherited the place of Communism as the basic instrument of violent change." This means the violence and terrorism -- which we, at first, used to say: "we'll ascribe it to Communism" -- has ended now. The Islamic awakening, from Morocco to Indonesia, has been its heir. Did you notice how [he did that]?! He concludes his book with zealous, astounding phrases. We will mention [only] one of them. He says: "When America was weak and poor, two hundred years ago, our faith was our salvation." Did you notice?! "And, we must, as we enter our third century..." -- with regard to the age of America -- "and as we greet the next millennium, rediscover our faith and [breathe new] vitality into it". Therefore, even President Nixon believes in extreme fundamentalism. Of course, he is not called an extremist* because he is not a Muslim preacher.

* Sheikh Safar pronounces it متطرف in "pause."

## Selection 25

الرئيس بوش يقول مثنياً على جيري فولول الذي سنحدثكم عنه إن
شاء الله يقول بوش « أعتقد بكل أمانة أننا برجال من أمثال جيري
فولول فإن شيئاً فظيعاً كالابادة الجماعية لليهود لن يحدث ثانية »
هذا جيري فولول من الزعماء... أو هو أكبر زعيم الأصولية النصرانية
في العالم التي تنادي بعودة اليهود وبعودة المسيح ويقول ... وهو
صديق حميم لجورج بوش وجورج بوش في كتابه التطلع الى الامام
يقول ... يذكر أن جده كان قسيساً وأنه متدين وأنه هووأسرته يقرأون
الكتاب المقدس كل يوم وأنه وقع في ورطة لما كان سفيراً في الصين

كيف يعمّد بنته والتعميد لا يفعله من النصارى إلا المتدينون وكلام كثير يذكر هو بنفسه يعني لا نحن يا إخوان ننبه هنا لا نعني متدين أنه متمسك بكل شئ دينهم أصلا دين فضفاض دين مرن دين واسع لا يقوم على حقائق تفصيلية وإنما التزام عام فهو في حدود الالتزام العام الذي ترضى به الكنيسة ويرضى به رجال الدين يعتبر من المتدينين

President Bush says, praising Jerry Falwell whom we will talk about--God willing--Bush says: "I believe, in all honesty, that with men of the likes of Jerry Falwell a horrible thing like the mass murder of the Jews will not happen again." This Jerry Falwell is one of the leaders ... or he is the greatest leader of Christian fundamentalism in the world which calls for the return of the Jews [to Zion] and the return of the Messiah. He says ... and he is a close friend of George Bush. And George Bush, in his book *Looking to the Future,* says .... He mentions that his grandfather was a minister; that he is a religious man, and that he and his family read the Holy Bible every day. [He also says] that he fell into a dilemma when he was ambassador to China. How would he baptize his daughter? (Only the very religious among the Christians practice baptism.) He talks a lot about himself. I mean, we are not, O brethren, pointing out here ... we do not mean [when we say] "extremely religious" that he is devoted to everything. Their religion is, at root, loose, a flexible religion, a broad religion. It does not rest upon detailed truths about things but rather a general commitment. He, within the general commitments' limits, with whom the church is pleased and [whom] the clergymen find acceptable, is considered as a highly religious person.

## Selection 26

كيف نشأت الحركة الصهيونية التي تطالب وتعد بأن أرض فلسطين أرضاً يهودية ومن أين جاء الشعور للعالم بأن الوعد الذي وعد الله تبارك وتعالى لابراهيم هو لليهود وليس للمسلمين ؟ الذي نسمع عنه وقرأناه في التاريخ أن الذي بدأ هذه الدعوى هو هرتزل هو اليهود والحقيقة غير ذلك . أول من بدأ الدعوة لتجميع اليهود ولتصديق نبؤات التوراة هم النصارى قبل اليهود وقبل الحركة الصهيونية بأكثر من أربعة قرون هذه هي الحقيقة التي إلا أن لم

نعيها جيداً فإننا لا نستطيع أن نقدر ونعرف مواقف الغرب وأمريكا
خاصة من الصراع الذي نحن نعيش فيه الآن

How did the Zionist Movement, which demands that -- and promises [that] -- the land of Palestine [should] be a Jewish land, spring up? Whence did the world come to have the feeling that the Promise which God, may He be blessed and exalted, made to Abraham is to the Jews and not to the Muslims? What we hear about, and [what] we've read in history, is that the one who began this call was Herzl, the Jew. But the truth is other than that. The first who began the call for the ingathering of the Jews and for giving credence to the prophecies of the Torah are the Christians, before the Jews and before the Zionist Movement by more than four centuries. This is the truth which, if we do not keep it well mind, we will not be able to evaluate and understand the positions of the West, especially America, on the conflict through which we are living now.

## Selection 27

فقام لوثر صاحب الحركة وترجم التوراة إلى اللغة الالمانية وكذلك
تُرجمت إلى اللغة الانجليزية . فانتشرت الحركة البروتستنتية كما
تعلمون أكثر ما انتشرت في المانيا وفي بريطانيا . فعندئذ آمن
هؤلاء بحرفية الكتاب المقدس وعصمة التوراة وأن كل حرف من
التوراة فهو وحي وحق من عند الله . فبدأوا يقرؤون مثل الوعد الذي
قرأنا لابراهيم وليعقوب . فكانت النتيجة أنه بظهور الحركة
البروتستنتية أخذ النصارى يؤمنون بأن أرض فلسطين حق لليهود .
فبدأت العلاقة تتحسن مع اليهود تدريجياً

So, Luther, the founder of the [Protestant] movement, up and translated the Torah into the German language, and it was also translated into the English language. And, the Protestant movement spread, as you know, as widely as it was to in Germany and Britain. At that time, those [people] believed in a literalist [understanding of] the Holy Bible and in the infallibility of the Torah; and [they also believed] that every letter of the Torah is a revelation and truth from God. So, they began to read the like of the promise, which we have read, to Abraham and to Jacob. The result was that, with the appearance of the Protestant Movement, Christians began to believe that the land of Palestine belongs to the Jews. And, the relationship with the Jews began to get better gradually.

## Selection 28

لما دخلوا أمريكا قالوا هذا خروج كخروج بني إسرائيل ودخولهم إلى الارض المقدسة . لاحظتم كيف شبهوا هذا بهذا ؟ وأخذوا يسمون المدن والاماكن التي في أمريكا باسماء من التوراة . وترسخت في أذهان المجتمع الامريكي أنكم الآن على التوراة وأن هذا بشرى بشركم الله بها . وهناك كلام كثير يضيق الوقت عن نقله لبعض الامريكان أو لمفكريهم يقولون إن هذه هي الارض الموعودة . حتى بعضهم قال ليست الارض ... اه ... أرض المسيح ليست فلسطين أرض المسيح هي أمريكا التي وعد الله تعالى بها. وسكنوا في أمريكا فتأسس المجتمع الامريكي على أفكار البروتستنت التي تنفي الكنيسة والواسطة وتؤمن بحرفية الكتاب المقدس

When [the Protestants] entered America, they said: "This Exodus [of ours from Europe] is like the Jews' Exodus [from Egypt] and [like] their entry into the Holy Land!" Have you noticed how they compared the former to the latter? And they began calling cities and places which are in America by names from the Torah. [The idea] that you were now [living] according to the Torah, and that this was "Good News" with which God had blessed you, became deeply rooted in the mind of American society. There is a great deal of discourse, which time is too tight to convey, from some Americans, or from their intellectuals, [who] say: "this is the Promised Land." Some of them even said: "The land ... ahh ... the land of the Messiah is not Palestine; the land of the Messiah is America about which God, may He be exalted, [made his] promise. They settled in America, and American society was founded on Protestant ideas which reject the [Catholic] church [hierarchy] and "intermediation" and [which] believe in the literal [truth of] the Holy Bible.

## Selection 29

في ... أثناء نهضة الحركة البروتستنتية في بريطانيا وفي أمريكا خاصة في القرن الماضي بدأت الفكرة الصهيونية تترعرع ووجدت الفكرة والحركة الصهيونية وتسمى الصهيونية النصرانية تمييزاً لها عن الصهيونية اليهودية التي دُعي إليها هرتزل وأتباعه كما نعلم مثلا نضرب أمثلة فقط سريعة في بريطانيا أُنشئ صندوق اكتشاف

فلسطين أيام الملكة فكتورية وكان رئيس الصندوق هو رئيس أساقفة كنتربري أكبر الاساقفة في بريطانيا هو رئيس هذا الصندوق ومهمته اكتشاف أرض الميعاد وحدود أرض الميعاد كما في التوراة ثم ظهر بعد ذلك بالفور. بالفور صاحب الوعد هذا المشهور تقول مؤرخة حياته ابنة أخته إنه كان يؤمن إيمانا عميقا بالتوراة ويقرأها ويصدق بها حرفيا وإنه نتيجة إيمانه بالتوراة أصدر هذا الوعد

During the revival of the Protestant movement in Britain and in America, especially the last century, the idea of Zionism began to flourish, and the Zionist ideology and movement were established. It is called Christian Zionism, to distinguish it from the Jewish Zionism to which Herzl and his followers were called, as we know. An example --we'll cite only a few quick examples -- in England the "Palestine Exploration Fund" was established in the days of Queen Victoria. The president of this fund was the Archbishop of Canterbury, the greatest of the Archbishops in Britain. He was the head of the fund, and its mission was to explore the Promised Land and the Promised Land's borders as in the Torah. Then, after that, Balfour appeared. Balfour is the author of this famous "Declaration." His biographer, his niece, says: "He believed deeply in the Torah, and used to read it. He took it literally, and as a result of his belief in the Torah, he issued this 'Declaration.'"

## Selection 30

قبل اشتداد عود اليهود كان النصارى أنفسهم مؤمنين بما يريدون أن يحققوه لإسرائل اليوم

Before the Jews' strength increased, the Christians, themselves, were believers in that which the [Jews] want to achieve for Isreal today.

## Selection 31

كانت هذه النتيجة يا إخوان نتيجة هذه الحركة البروتستنتية التي كان منها هؤلاء الرجال الذين ذكرنا أن ظهرت في أمريكا صحوة دينية عجيبة . نعم إنها صحوة . ويسمونها صحوة . ويسمونها أصولية — الصحوة الاصولية أو الانجيلية . ويؤمن أفرادها بهذه الوعود أو هذا الوعد وبضرورة قيام دولة إسرائيل ومساعدة دولة إسرائيل والقضاء على المسلمين

This result was, O brothers... the result of this Protestant Movement (of which these men whom we have mentioned were a part]) was that an amazing religious awakening appeared in America. Yes, it is an awakening. And, they call it an "Awakening." They call it "Fundamentalism" -- the "Fundamentalist" or "Evangelical" awakening. And, its members believe in these promises, or this promise, and in the necessity of establishing the state of Israel, in supporting the state of Israel, and in eliminating the Muslims.

## Selection 32

يجب أن نعي جيداً أننا مغفلون نحن المسلمين ومستغفلون من قبل وسائل إعلامنا التي لا تعطينا هذا الوجه الحقيقي الذي يتكاثر ويتنامى كل يوم في أمريكا بلاد العلمانية والاباحية وبلاد الالحاد . ولكن مع ذلك فيها هذا الاتجاه وفيها هذه الصحوة

We must realize well that we are fools, we Muslims. We are being fooled by our news media which does not give us this true perspective which is growing and developing everyday in America, the land of secularism, permissiveness, and atheism. But, in spite of that, there is this tendency there, and there is this awakening there.

## Selection 33

أولاً الامريكان ليسوا شعباً غير متدين كما قد يبدوا لنا لكن كما قلت وأؤكد ذلك الدين عندهم دين عام دين فضفاض دين مرن يكفي أن ترتبط بالكنيسة فتكون متديناً وتؤمن بما تقوله الكنيسة وما تعد به وما تقرره . هذا المقصود لا يعني ذلك السلوك الجاد لكن نقول في إحصائيات عالمية أجريت تبين من بين الدول النصرانية أن أكثر الشعوب النصرانية في العالم تديناً من حيث النسبة العددية أولاً إيرلاندا ثم تأتي بعدها أمريكا . ويذكر معهد جالوب متخصص هو في الاحصائيات أن أكثر من ٩٤٪ من سكان الولايات المتحدة الامريكية يؤمنون بالله . يعني عملوا استبيانات كبيرة جداً

First, the Americans are not an irreligious people as it might seem to us; but as I said -- and I reaffirm it -- religion is, with them, a generalized religion, a loose religion, a flexible religion. It suffices that you join a church to be religious; [it is enough that] you believe in what the church says, promises and stipulates; this is the objective. That does not mean serious behavior. But, we can say, through international statistics which have been taken, it has become clear that, among the Christian states, the most religious people in the world, as a percentage of population, is first Ireland. Then, after it comes America. The Gallup Institute -- it specializes in statistics -- says that more than 94% of the population of the United States believe in God. I mean [Gallup] has done very large surveys.

## Selection 34

نذكر بإيجاز كم عدد مدارس — المدارس الدينية — في أمريكا ؟ كم عددها ؟ كم تتوقعون ؟ والجامعات والشبكات التلفزيونية ؟ كم؟ أتظنون أن الصحوة النصرانية في أمريكا مثل الصحوة الاسلامية عندنا ليس لها مجلة ولا جريدة ولا إذاعة فضلاً عن قناة تلفزيونية بالأقمار الصناعية ؟ أتظنون ذلك ؟ انظروا كيف يكون ! ماذا عند الامريكيين ! وماذا عند علماء دينهم ! تمتلك الكنائس — أنا أقرأ الآن — وتدير عدة مئات من المعاهد والكليات والجامعات في الولايات المتحدة الامريكية . في عام ١٩٨١ و١٩٨٢ — لاحظوا عشرة سنوات هذا الكلام — بلغ عدد معاهد التعليم العالى ١٩٧٨ معهداً . يعني الآن

خلوها بس صارت كم ألفين معهد . أما المدارس فإنها بعد أن كانت في عام ١٩٥٤ و١٩٥٥ كان عددها لا يزيد عن ١٢٣ مدرسة أصبح عددها في عام ١٩٨٠. يزيد عن ١٨ ألف مدرسة .

Let us talk briefly ... what is the number of schools -- religious schools -- in America? How many are there? How many do you expect? And universities and television networks? How many? Do you think that the Christian awakening in America is like our Islamic awakening here -- not having a single magazine, nor a newspaper, nor a radio station, let alone a television channel via satellite? Do you think that? Just look how it is! What the Americans have! What their religious scholars have! The churches own --I'm reading now-- and administer many hundreds of institutes, colleges, and universities in the United States of America. In the years 1981 and '82 -- See?! Ten years [ago], this statement! -- the number of institutes of higher education amounted to one thousand nine hundred seventy eight. I mean, now, let's say they've only become two thousand institutes. But [elementary] schools! While their number was, in 1954 and1955, not more than 123, that number came to be, in the year 1980, more than eighteen thousand!

## Selection 35

ومن الادلة التي يستدل الباحثون والمحللون على تدين أمريكا وعودتها إلى المحافظة أنها اختارت آخر رئيسين قبل بوش من المتدينين المحافظين وهما كارتر وريغان . فكارتر كان منتمياً وملتزما إلتزاماً واضحاً بالكنيسة الانجيلية ولا يزال كارتر إلى هذا اليوم مبشراً ويتنقل من أفغانستان إلى الحبشة إلى السودان ويمر بهذه البلاد أحيانا ويذهب في كل مكان يدافع عن التنصير وينشر قضية النصرانية .

One of the pieces of evidence which researchers and analysts into America's religiosity and return to conservatism cite is that it chose its last two presidents, before Bush, from among religious conservatives, they being Carter and Reagan. Carter was a member of and clearly committed to the Evangelical Church, and Carter is, to this very day, a preacher. He travels from Afghanistan to Ethiopia and Sudan. Sometimes, he passes through these countries and goes everywhere defending Christian missionarism and spreading Christianity's message.

## Selection 36

نجئ إلى دلائل اغرب وأعجب من هذا كله وهي ما أثر الدينفي الاعلام الامريكي — محطات الاذاعة ومحطات التليفزيون وكلها دائما تفتح وتتحدث عن التوراة ورجالها ؟ يقول احتلت صور النجوم — نجوم البرامج الدينية المسموعة والمرئية أمثال بيلي جراهم وجيري فولول — صفحات أبرز المجلات الاسبوعية . وأصبحت تسيطر على عقول الامريكيين حتى أن هؤلاء النجوم ومنهم اسواجرط — معروف عند الجميع لأنه ... ( معروف بماذا اسواجرط ؟ مناظراته عديدات نعم) — فجيمي اسواجرط أحد هؤلاء النجوم كما سنذكر أصبحوا ... أصبح هؤلاء النجوم — نجوم الأصولية الامريكية — ينافسون نجوم السينما ونجوم الرياضة والفن في أمريكا بكثرة من ينظر اليهم ويتتبع أخبارهم وأحاديثهم

We [now] come to [even] stranger and more amazing evidence than all of that, it being: what is the effect of religion on the American media -- radio stations and television stations, all of which always make an opening statement on the Torah and its personalities? They say [that] pictures of the stars -- the stars of religious radio and TV programs like Billy Graham and Jerry Falwell -- have taken over the pages of the most famous weekly magazines. [Those stars] have come to control the minds of Americans so much so that those stars, among them Swaggert -- he's known to everyone because he ... (what is he famous for, Swaggert? His controversies are many, yes!) -- Therefore, Jimmy Swaggert, one of those stars, as we will mention, have ... has ... these stars [have] come to -- the stars of American fundamentalism -- compete with movie stars and the stars of sports and art in America, because of the large number of those who watch them and follow news of them and their talks.

## Selection 37

يقول جيمي اسواجرط — خذوا مقطع واحد فقط شاهد يا إخوان من كلام اواسجرط — هذا عن عقيدته بالنسبة لاسرائيل وهو صاحب محطة من اكبر المحطات وشبكة عظيمة جداً من الاذاعات والصحافة أيضا يقول « أشعر أن الولايات المتحدة الامريكية مرتبطة بحبل ولادة سري مع إسرائيل وتعود هذه الروابط في اعتقادي إلى ما قبل

ظهور الولايات المتحدة الامريكية بزمن طويل كما ترجع الفكرة اليهودية المسيحية إلى ابراهيم ووعد الرب له وهو وعد أعتقد أنه يشمل الولايات المتحدة الامريكية أيضاً >> يعني وعد الرب يشمل أيضاً امريكا << لأن الله ما زال يقول -- إني أبارك الذين يباركون إسرائيل وألعن من يلعنونها — ومن فضل الله على الولايات المتحدة الامريكية أنها ما زالت قوية اليوم وأنا واثق أن هذا يعود إلى كونها تقف وراء إسرائيل وادعو الله أن نظل دوماً سنداً لاسرائيل >>

Jimmy Swaggert says -- take just one passage as evidence, brothers, from this discourse of Swaggert's about his belief regarding Israel, he being the owner of one of the biggest stations and a very big broadcasting network and press as well. He says: "I feel that the United States of America is connected by a secret umbilical cord with Israel. These links go back, according to my belief, to before the appearance of the United States of America by a long while, just as Judeo-Christian thought goes back to Abraham and the Lord's Promise to him. It is a promise that, I believe, includes the United States of America as well." That means, the Lord's promise includes America also. "[This is] because God still says: 'I will bless those who bless Israel, and I will curse those who curse them.' Because of God's blessing of the United States of America, it is still strong today, and I am confident that this is because it stands by Israel; I pray God that we always continue to support Israel."

## Selection 38

أشهر هذه القيادات وأعظمهم أثراً هو المدعو جيري فولول صاحب المنظمة التي يسمونها << منظمة الاغلبية الاخلاقية>> أو << الاغلبية المعنوية .>> يقول من كلماته << إن دعم الولايات المتحدة الامريكية لاسرائيل ليس من أجل مصلحة إسرائيل لا>> كيف ؟ قال << ولكن من أجل مصلحة الولايات المتحدة الامريكية نفسها >> هذا الرجل ... يعني عجيب جداً... ظهر بدعوة طويلة جداً في أمريكا عريضة تقول << إن الولايات المتحدة الامريكية يجب أن تكون أمة مسيحية >> وبعد أن ظهر له شعبية وإذا به يقلب هذه الدعوة ويغير هذا الشعار ويقول << إن الولايات المتحدة الامريكية جمهورية مسيحية يهودية >>

The most famous one in this [religious] leadership, and the most influential, is the one called Jerry Falwell, the head of the organization which they call the "Moral Majority" (or "Morale Majority") Organization. He says, in his own words: "The United States of America's support for Israel is not in the interest of Israel. No!" How [can that be?!] He said: "But, rather it is in the interest of the United States of America itself!" This man ... I mean, it's very strange ... has conducted a very extensive and broad mission in America which says: "The United States of America must be a Christian nation!" But after he became popular, all of a sudden, he turns this mission upside down and changes this slogan saying: " The United States of America is a Christian-Jewish Republic!"

## Selection 39

ويقول فولول << إن الوقوف ضد إسرائيل هو وقوف ضد الله >>

Falwell says: "To stand against Israel is to stand against God!"

## Selection 40

هذا ما يقول هذا الرجل الذي يهاجم في كثير من محطاته الاذاعية
الكثيرة جداً يهاجم العرب ويقول << لا مكان للعرب بيننا ولا علاقة
حسنة معهم لأنهم ينكرون قيم الولايات المتحدة الامريكية وطريقة
معيشتها ويرفضون الاعتراف بإسرائيل >>

This is what this man, who attacks -- on many of his very many broadcasting stations -- (he attacks the Arabs), is saying. He says: "There is no place for the Arabs among us, nor [can there be any] good relationship with them, because they reject the values of the United States of America and its way of life. And, they refuse to recognize Israel."

## Selection 41

أعلن بات روبرتسن نفسه عام ١٩٨٨— ايش أعلن؟ — أنه مرشح
لرئاسة الولايات المتحدة الامريكية . وكاد أن ينافس الرئيس بوش
في الانتخابات ولكنه انسحب بعد ذلك . انظر حتى تعرفوا يعني ما
يتمتع به من نفوذ وهو من القادة الاصوليين المتطرفين في أمريكا .
يعني السياسة حرام على الاصوليين الاسلاميين فقط

Pat Robertson declared himself, in 1988.... What did he declare? That he was a candidate for the Presidency of the United States of America. And, he almost competed with President Bush in the presidential elections, but he withdrew after that. Just look, so you'll know, I mean, how much influence he enjoys, he being one of the leaders of the extreme fundamentalists in America. That means politics is prohibited only to Islamic fundamentalists!

## Selection 42

في افتتاح هذه المحطة التي تغطي سورية والعراق وتركيا ومصر
وشمال الجزيرة العربية — كلها تغطيها هذه المحطة التلفزيونية —
يقول هذا الخبيث في افتتاحها << لا يسد القرآن والتعاليم الاسلامية
أعمق حاجات الروح الانسانية >> افتتحها بمهاجمة القرآن الكريم <<
هذه هي أيام عصيبة حيث يستند الاسلام إلى عقيدة منقسمة >> ذيك
الايام ترون طبعاً الشيعة والسنة والصراعات يقول هذه عقيدة
منقسمة الاسلام وانتهى أمره وتتطلع الشيوعية أو المادية طلباً للاجابة
يعني في نظر بات روبرسن تسقط الشيوعية ويسقط الاسلام والذي
يعلو هو نجم الانجيلية الاصولية التي يدعو إليها . يقول << ومع
وجود مشاعر سلبية عميقة لدى المسلمين>> — شوفو كيف؟ — <<
فهناك انفتاح جديد عندهم لتقبل رسالة الانجيل إذا ما قدمت اليهم
بواسطة التلفزيون >>

In an opening statement for [Pat Robertson's Middle East TV station in south Lebanon], which covers Syria, Iraq, Turkey, Egypt and the northern part of the Arabian Peninsula -- this television station covers all of [that] -- this loathsome [person] says in his opening statement: "The Quran and Islamic teachings do not fulfill the deepest needs of the human spirit." He opened [the station] by attacking the Glorious Qur'an! "These are critical days when Islam is based upon a divided faith." These days you do see, of course, the Shi'ah, the Sunnah and conflicts [between Muslims], so he says this is a divided faith, Islam. "Its influence has ended, and Communism or materialism are casting about seeking some sort of positive response." That means, from Pat Robertson's viewpoint, Communism is falling and Islam is falling, and the thing that will rise is the star of Fundamentalist Evangelism which he calls for. He says: "Despite the existence of deep negative feelings among Muslims..." (See how [he thinks!]) "... there is a new openness among them to accept the Evangelical message when it is presented to them through television."

## Selection 43

أيها الاخوة الموضوعات الحقيقة والفقرات كثيرة ولكن أحب أن أقول إن الذين يؤمنون بهذا الوعد التوراتي هم يؤمنون بالمسيح الدجال . وبالتالى كل من يعتقد أو يوافق على مشروع لبقاء إسرائيل آمنة مطمئنة فإنه شاء أم أبى علم أو لم يعلم هو يعمل لهدف إنشاء مملكة الدجال هذه . ويسعي لتحقيق النبوءة التوراتية التي يدعيها هؤلاء وإنه يخدم راضيا أو غير راض يعلم أو لا يعلم هذه الاهداف الصهيونية التي يؤمن بها هؤلاء الاصوليون مع أولئك اليهود

O brothers, the[se] topics, it is true, and the[se] paragraphs are many, but I would like to say that those who believe in this Torah promise believe in the false Messiah. And subsequently, everyone who believes in or agrees with any plan to leave Israel secure and tranquil -- whether he likes it or not, whether he knows it or not -- he is working towards the goal of establishing the kingdom of this false [Messiah]. He is striving to implement the Torah prophecy which these [people] assert. He is serving -- like it or not, knowingly or unknowingly -- these Zionist aims in which those fundamentalists believe along with those Jews.

## Selection 44

وقد رفع النصارى رؤوسهم وبدأوا يقولون إن أحداث الخليج هيئت لنا
الفرصة لادخال دين المسيح في مناطق لم نكن نحلم أن ندخلها فيها من
قبل والتنصير يا إخوان علني والكنائس علنية ومؤيدة علنا في
الكويت في الامارات في البحرين وموجود بشكل كثيف أيضا
تنصير خبيث في اليمن وفي عمان والاردن -- الاردن مندوبها في
مؤتمر مدريد نصراني -- وفيها تخطيط تنصيري رهيب إذاً كلنا الآن
كل البلاد محاطة بالتنصير فالبلد الذي يريدون أن ينصروه والعياذ
بالله ولن يكون ذلك إن شاء الله هو هذه البلاد

The Christians have become optimistic; they have started to say: " The events of the Gulf have provided a chance for us to introduce the religion of the Messiah into regions which we never dreamed that we might enter before." Christian missionarism, O brothers, is [done in the] open! Churches [operate in the] open and are supported openly in Kuwait, in the United Arab Emirates, and in Bahrain. There is to be found, in an intensive form too, a loathsome Christian missionary activity in Yemen, Oman, and in Jordan -- Jordan, its representative at the Madrid Conference is a Christian! -- there is a frightful plan for Christian missionary work. Therefore, all of us are now -- all the countries -- surrounded by Christian missionarism. The country they want [most] to Christianize -- [all] refuge is in God, and it will not happen, God willing -- is this country.

## Selection 45

ونعلن إسلامية المعركة بكل قوة مؤتمر مدريد مثلا هذا المؤتمر كغيره
من المؤتمرات لم يُمثل فيه الاسلام لم يُقَل فيه << قال الله >> ولا << قال
رسول الله >> ولم يُقَل فيه << إن القدس أرض إسلامية >> إذاً هذه
قضيتنا الاساسية نحن لا ننظر إلى الجدل العقيم في النتائج
والتوقعات ننظر إلى أساس القضية . القضية إسلامية دينية لا تخص
الفلسطينيين ولا العرب ولا حتى المسلمين المعاصرين اليوم بل هي
قضية إسلامية تهم كل المسلمين إ......لى قيام الساعة

# Chapter Two

We declare the Islamicness of the battle with all [our] strength! The Madrid Conference, for instance, this Madrid Conference is like other conferences; Islam is not represented at it! "God said" or "the Prophet of God said" are never spoken at it! "Jerusalem is Islamic land" is never said at it! Therefore, this is our Islamic issue. We are not looking at the sterile struggle for "results" and "expectations"; we look at the root of the issue! The issue is Islamic, religious. It does not concern the Palestinians, the Arabs or even the contemporary Muslims of today, but rather it is an Islamic issue which concerns all the Muslims until the [last] hour strikes.

# Chapter Three

# Women

## Introduction

The status of women is one of the "indicator" questions in contemporary discourse between the "Left" and the "Right." "Conservatives" and "liberals," whether they be secularists, Christians, Jews or Muslims (to mention only those who concern us directly here) within their respective religions or across the lines of worldview find more to divide over than to agree upon when discussing the topic as we endlessly do. The following selections are from Sheikh Safar al-Hawali's "lesson" entitled دفاع عن المرأة -- "A Defense of Woman."

# Chapter Three

**"External and Internal Abuses"** from ***A Defense of Woman*** by **Safar al-Hawali.**

## Selection 1

عنوان هذا الدرس « دفاع عن المرأة » وكنت وعدتكم أن عنوانه « نحو جماعة إسلامية واحدة » ولكن هذا الموضوع الأخير يحتاج إلى تأمل وتدبر وشورى فأجلته أسابيع

The title of this lesson is "A Defense of Woman." I had promised you that its title would be "Towards One Islamic Society." But, this latter topic needs a deep look and organization and consultation, so I delayed it for a few weeks.

## Selection 2

أما أسباب هذا الدرس فثلاثة أسباب . الأول لأن المرأة أصبحت مستهدفة وطريقًا للغزو ونافذة للتأثير الحضاري وأصبحت لعبة بيد المهرّجين والمروّجين ينفّذون منها إلى قعر دار الإسلام . الثاني اتهام الإسلام من قبل أعدائه أنه حجر على المرأة حقول المشاركة وحجّمها وقلّص دورها في الحياة الدنيا وأنه سبب تعاستها اتعسهم الله . الثالث تقصير كثير من الناس في حقوق المرأة والتهاون بشأنها الخطير ومكانتها السامقة

As for the reasons for this lesson, there are three reasons. The first is because woman has become a target, an open road for attack, and a window for cultural influence. She has become a plaything in the hands of the obscene and the rumor-mongers trying to penetrate, using her, into the very depths of the Abode of Islam. The second [reason] is the accusation against Islam, by its enemies, that it has closed, against woman, fields of participation, secluded her, and diminished her role in worldly life; that *it* is the reason for her misery, may God make them miserable. The third [reason] is the restriction by many people of woman's rights and [their] disdain for her serious position and her lofty status.

## Selection 3

والمعنى أن المرأة شقيقة الرجل وأنها نصف المجتمع وأنها المؤدية للرسالة في بنات جنسها . والمرأة عندنا أم وزوجة وبنت وأخت ومعلمة ومربية وداعية . قال سبحانه وهو يتفضل على عباده في العمل الصالح << إن المسلمين والمسلمات والمؤمنين والمؤمنات>> فذكر الله أفعال الخيرحتى ختم الأية ويقول سبحانه وتعالى في سورة آل عمران يوم ذكر الدعاة والمجاهدين والعاملين والمهاجرين << فاستجاب لهم ربهم أني لا أضيع عمل عادل منكم من ذكر أو أنثى بعضكم من بعض >> وقال سبحانه وتعالى << والمؤمنون والمؤمنات بعضهم من بعض >>

The meaning [of this] is that woman is the sister of man. She [makes up] half of society, and she is the fulfiller of the [Islamic] mission among the daughters of her gender. Woman is -- among us -- a mother, a wife, a daughter, a sister, a teacher, a nurturer, and a preacher. God, when encouraging his servants to good work, said: "Verily, Muslim men and Muslim women and believing men and believing women ...."* Then, God went on to mention good acts until the end of the verse. And, God, may He be glorified and exalted, says, in *Surat 'Al ᶜUmran* -- on the day he mentioned preachers and strugglers and workers and emigrants: "And, their Lord replied to them: 'I will not waste the act of any worker among you whether male or female, one of you or another.'"† And, He, may He be glorified and exalted, said: "And, believing men and believing women one of them or another."‡

* Qur'an 33:35; the insistence on both genders of the plural nouns is taken to show God's equal concern for both genders.

† Qur'an 31:195.

‡ Qur'an 9:71; the text actually reads بعضهم أولياء بعض not من as in the preceding citation.

## Selection 4

فالمراة أسيرة وجب على المسلم أن يرحمها وأن يقدّرها وأن يحترمها

Woman is a prisoner. The Muslim must be merciful towards her and honor her and respect her.

## Selection 5

لماذا نهتم بالمرأة ؟ لماذا ندافع عن المرأة ؟ لأنها مظلومة . ظلمت من المجتمع الجاهلي الوثني الشركي في الجزيرة العربية فحرموها الميراث والرأي وجعلوها عقيماً عن حمل المبادئ واستخفوا بها حتى عاملوها كما عاملتها الحضارة الغربية والثقافة المادية تماماً . ذكر ذلك ابوالحسن الندوي في كتابه ماذا خسر العالم بانحطاط المسلمين فأي مصيبة حلت بالمرأة في جاهليتها مصيبة دهياء لايعلمها إلا الله . ومظلومة من الوضع الكافر الذي نعيشه الآن . يوم أخرج المرأة بعد الحرب العالمية الثانية لتقود الدبابة وتكون طيارة وتأخذ السلاح وتحمل الكلاشنكوف تصارع الأبطال والكتائب وتقاتل في ساحة المعركة وتكون جندية مرور إنها والله أمور تدل على أنهم ما قدروا المرأة حق قدرها وأنهم خذلوها في أعظم شئ تملكه وهو العفاف والحياء والطهر والحياء

Why do we concern ourselves with woman? Why do we defend woman? Because she is unjustly treated. She is unjustly treated by the ignorant, pagan, polytheistic society of the Arabian peninsula. They have forbidden her [her legitimate] inheritance and [her right to express] an opinion; they have made her incapable of bearing [her] principles and degraded her so far as to have treated her exactly as Western civilization and materialist culture has treated her. Abu al-Hasan al-Nadawi mentioned that in his book *What has the World Lost in the Decline of the Muslims.* What a disaster has befallen woman in her ignorance! [She is] injured, in a disastrous state while only God knows it. And, [she is] unjustly treated by the infidel situation [in] which we now live. On the day [they] sent woman out, after the Second World War, to drive tanks and to be a pilot, to take up weapons and carry the Kalashnikov, to combat heroes and regiments and fight on the field of battle and be a traffic police officer, all these, by God, are matters which show that they have not respected woman as much as she is due. They have humiliated her in the greatest thing she possesses that being virtue, a sense of shame, purity and that sense of shame.

## Selection 6

والمرأة مظلومة من بعض الآباء . فإن كثير من الآباء لايعرفون قدر المرأة . فلا يستشيرونها ولا يعتبرون رأيها . ومنهم من كان حجر عثرة في زواج إبنته فإذا تقدم الكفء رفضه برأيه هو لا برأيها ولم يخبرها ويرفض زواجها حتى تعيش العنوسة واليبس والأسى

And, woman is unjustly treated by some fathers. Many fathers do not know woman's value. They do not seek her counsel and do not take her opinion into account. Among them is he who has been a stumbling block to his daughter's marriage. If an appropriate suitor comes forward, [the father] rejects him [relying on] his own opinion and not her's, not having informed her. Or, he refuses to give her in marriage such that she lives [in] spinsterhood, aridity, and grief.

## Selection 7

ومظلومة أيضاً من بعض الأزواج . فهو يتعامل معها كأنها دابّة في البيت . لا احترام لا رحمة لا سماع رأي لامناقشة بالتي هي أحسن لا إعطاء حقوق . وإنما هو يراها أنها من صنف آخر ويتعامل معها بفظاظة وغلظة . وسوف يأتي شئ من ذلك

And, [woman is] unjustly treated by some husbands. He [may] treat her as though she were an animal in the home. No respect, no mercy, no listening to [her] opinion no discussion of what is best, no giving [her her] rights. Rather, he deems her [to be] of some other, [lesser] kind [of being] and deals with her rudely and coarsely. Something [more] of that will come up [as we continue the discussion].

## Selection 8

الله عز وجل يدافع عن المرأة لان المرأة من المسلمين المؤمنين قال
سبحانه وتعالى << إن الله يدافع عن الذين آمنوا >> فالذي يدافع عن
المرأة أولاً هو رب العزة والجلال تبارك الله رب العالمين والرسول عليه
الصلاة والسلام يدافع عن المرأة فقد أعطاها حقوقها وسنّ لها صلى
الله عليه وسلم ما لها من حق في كثير من المناسبات يأتي تفصيل ذلك

God, most lofty and sublime, defends woman because woman is a Muslim and a believer. He, may He be glorified and exalted, said: "Verily God defends those who believe."* So, He who defends woman first is the Lord of glory and sublimity. May God, Lord of the universe, be blessed. And, His Prophet, upon him be blessings and peace, defends woman. He gave her her rights and enacted laws for her, may God grant him blessings and peace, [to have] that right which was her's, [doing so] on many occasions. The details of this will come up [again in our discussion].

* Qur'an 22:38.

## Selection 9

لكن هذا الجاهل وهذا الأحمق ظن أنه إذا ذكر المرأة أنه دنّس الأسماع أو
المجلس فيقول << المرأة أكرمكم الله >> وهذه كلمة خاطئة حرام أن
تُنطق وأن تقول ... أن تقال . وعلى من حضر المجلس وسمع هذا أن
ينكر بأشد الإنكار ويقول << لا ! تُذكر المرأة وهي كرامة تُحترم ولا بأس
أن يذكر اسمها >> كما سوف يأتي

But, this ignoramus and this fool has come to believe that, if he should mention woman, he would pollute the ears [of his companions] or the *majlis*,* so he says: "Woman, may God be kind to you."† But, this is a mistaken [use of the] word. It is forbidden that it be pronounced and that you should say ... that it should be said.‡ And, whoever has attended the *majlis* and heard this must denounce [it] in he strongest terms and say: "No! It is a token of honor [when] woman is mentioned. She is respected. There is no harm if her nam e is mentioned" as will come up [in further discussion].

* Qur'an 22:38.
† The مَجْلِس [*majlis*] here refers especially to a social get-together though the term has a wide range of meanings.
‡ I.e. as I have not by making any mention of a taboo subject.

## Selection 10

ومنها حرمان عند البعض من الميراث وهذه مأساة اجتماعية تعيشها المجتمعات القروية والبدوية والقبلية فيرون أن من العيب أن تذهب المرأة لتطلب ميراثها من أهلها ويندون بمن يفعل ذلك وهم المخطؤون وعلى هؤلاء أن يؤدبون تأديباً رادعاً يزجرهم وأمثالهم وأن تُرفع قضاياهم إلى القضاة الشرعيين حتى يؤخذ في صددهم الإجراء اللازم لأنهم خالفوا منهج الله وحكموا بحكم الشريعة ورفضوا الكتاب والسنة

And, among [those problems] is the deprivation [of women] by some [persons] of [their] inheritance. This is a social disaster which village, Bedouin and tribal groups confront. They believe that it is wrong that woman go to ask for her inheritance of her family, and they criticize those who do that. But, they are mistaken. They must be corrected with a deterrent which will restrain them and their likes; their actions must be brought before judges in law such that the necessary procedure be taken against them because they have contravened God's way and held against the *Shari<sup>c</sup>ah*'s rulings and rejected the Book and the *Sunnah*.

## Selection 11

الميراث حق للمرأة . لم يتولَه نبي مرسل ولا ملَك مقرّب ولا عالم من العلماء وإنما تولاه الله بنفسه فأعطى كل ذي حق حقه فله الحمد وله الشكر. يا أيها الإخوة بعض الناس الآن حرم قريبته خالته بنته أخته من الميراث وإذا ذهبت تأخذ الميراث شنّ عليها أهل الحي والقبيلة والقرية . وهؤلاء مخطؤون . والواجب أن نرفع هذا الخطأ وهذا الحظر

السئ القبيح الذي أصبح وصمة عار في وِجوه أهل الإسلام . لابد أن تعطى مباشرة حتى ولو رفضت . تجبر وهي تحاول أن تُعطى . ويذهب المعصّب أو القريب يذهب بنفسه ليعرض عليها حقها الذي أحقه الله سبحانه وتعالى لها

Inheritance is woman's right. No prophet sent or favored angel nor any scholar has taken responsibility for it [from her.] Rather God Himself has taken responsibility for it. He has given his right to every one who has the right, so praise be to Him and thanks be to Him. O brothers, some people now have forbidden their female relative -- their maternal aunt, their daughter, their sister -- [her] inheritance. If she goes to get the inheritance, the people of the neighborhood, the tribe, or the village attack her. These [people] are mistaken. It is [our] duty to point up this mistake, this bad, ugly prohibition which has become a token of shame on the faces of the people of Islam. [Woman] must be given [her inheritance] directly even if she has rejected [it]. She must be forced -- [even] while trying [to refuse it] -- to be given [the inheritance]. The *mu$^{c}$assib* * should go; or [her] relative should go, himself, to offer to her [that] due which God, may He be glorified and exalted, has authorized for her.

* The person within a family or community charged with managing peoples' needs. Lit. "he who bandages/binds" [i.e. societal wounds] or "he whose eyes are covered/blindfolded" [i.e. can act impartially?].

## Selection 12

تحجيم دورها فقط في الولادة والإنجاب — يفهم بعض الجهلاء أن دور المرأة فقط أن تنجب وأن تحمل وأن تضع فقط وأن ترضع . أما غير ذلك من حياتها فليس لها مجال في ذلك . وهذا خطأ . لها التربية ولها أن تعلم بنات جنسها ولها أن تدعو ولها أن تشارك برأيها ولها كذلك أن تشارك بدعائها ولها أن تقوم على أطفالها ولها أن تخرج العلماء والزعماء والأدباء والقادة والشهداء والصالحين إلى غير ذلك مما سوف أذكره

Restricting her role solely to bearing and producing [children] -- Some of the ignorant understand that woman's role is only to conceive, bear, ... and bring forth [children] only ... and to nurse. As for anything else in her life, there is no place for her in [any of] that. And, that is wrong. She has child rearing, and it's up to her to educate others of her gender; it's up to her to proselytize and to share her opinion. It's up to her, as well, to participate in her missionary activity. She has to supervise her children and to produce scholars, leaders, literati, commanders, martyrs and doers of good deeds and so on which I will [go on to] mention.

## Selection 13

كأنهم لا يتصورن أن لها طاقة محدودة وأنها ضعيفة وأنها تحمل وتضع وأنها تعاني الأمرين فتشارك في الحراثة والزراعة وفي الإحتطاب وفي رعي الأغنام وفي حمل الأثقال وفي صنع الطعام وفي كنس البيت وفي غير ذلك حتى تبقى تعمل الساعات الطويلة من العمل المضني الذي لا يعمله إلا عمال المناجم في مناجم الفحم أو مناجم استخراج الذهب والفضه . وهذا لم يقره الإسلام . لهن طاقة وهي إمرأة ضعيفة

[For others] it is as though they cannot imagine that she has limited strength; that she is weak; that she bears [children] and brings them forth; that she suffers both matters and then shares in plowing, and planting, and gathering firewood, and herding sheep, and in carrying heavy loads, and preparing food, and in sweeping the house, and so on until she goes on working for long hours of exhausting work which only mine workers in coal mines or gold and silver extraction mines do. This, Islam has not laid it out. They have [only] a [limited] capacity [to do all this] while being a weak woman.

## Selection 14

قال صلى الله عليه وسلم يقول << الله الله في النساء>> والمعنى في ضعفهن . فإنهن ضعيفات لايستطعن حمل كثير من الأمور . لكن المجتمع الجاهلي قد يكيّف المرأة لأن تحمل عملاً من الأعمال ويجدها مقصّرة إذا لم تقم بهذا العمل . فتجد الرجل يثرّب على امرأته إذا ما رآها تحرث وتزرع وتحمل الحبوب وترعي الأغنام وتحتطب وتذهب وتأتي وتستقي وتفعل أفعالاً كثيرة لايفعلها أربعة عمال أو خمسة عمال . والاسلام لم يأتِ بهذا أبداً . وهذا ظلم لها لايقره دين الله

[The Prophet, Muhammad], may God bless him and grant him peace, said: "[O] God [O] God [what] about women!" The meaning [of that has to do] with their weakness. They really are weak; they cannot bear many matters. But, pagan society can condition woman to bear a certain [amount of] work and then find her inferior if she does not carry out the task. You'll find man rebuking his wife if he does not see her plowing, and planting, and carrying grain, and herding sheep, and gathering firewood, and coming and going, and drawing water, and doing [so] many things [that] four laborers or five [could] not do them. Islam never brought this [into the world]. This is injustice against her which God's religion does not acknowledge.

### Selection 15

حرمانها من التعليم في بعض الجهات -- والتعليم عندنا بمواصفات إسلامية تحت مظلة « إياك نعبد واياك نستعين » أن تُعلم المرأة ما يقوم بشئون دينها ما يقرّبها من الله ما يجعلها خائفة متقية متحجبة محتشمة في هذا الحدود وقد علم الرسول عليه الصلاة والسلام الصحابيات

Forbidding her instruction in some quarters -- Education, with us, is among Islamic specifications under the umbrella of [the Qur'anic dictum]: "Thee do we worship and of Thee do we seek help." That woman [should be] instructed [in] that which has to do with matters of her religion, that which will bring her closer to God, that which will make her [God] fearing, pious, veiled, and modest lies within these limits. The Prophet, upon him be blessings and peace, taught the women Companions.

### Selection 16

قضية أن تبقى المرأة جاهلة لاتجوّد القرآن ولاتحفظ كتاب الله عز وجل ولاتعرف السنة ولا الفقه . قضية خاطئة نرفضها . قضية التعليم الفاضح الذي يدعوا المرأة إلى أن تشارك الرجل في البرلمان وأن تشاركه في حقول الحياة وأن تخرج متبدلة متكشفة سافرة نرفضه

ونعتبر أنه تعليم جاهلي لايزيدها إلا ردى ويقودها إلى النار . نريد تعليمًا إسلاميًا موقّرًا مقدّسًا طاهرًا يقودها إلى جنة عرضها السموات والأرض . كانت عائشة رضي الله عنها عالمة وأقل ما تحفظ من الشعر - - قال الزهري كانت عائشة تحفظ من الشعر ثمانية عشر الف بيت من الشعر

[It is] a problem that woman remains ignorant: not reciting the Qur'an properly; not memorizing the Book of God, glorified and magnified be He; not knowing the *Sunnah* nor *fiqh*. [It is] a mistaken problem which we reject. [As for] the problem of that scandalous education which calls upon woman to join man in parliament; to join him in the [various] fields of life; to go out transformed, exposed, unveiled -- we reject it! We consider it to be a pagan education which will only expose her to more ruin and lead her to Hell-fire. We want an Islamic, dignified, sanctified, pure education which will lead her to Paradise whose realm is both the heavens and the earth. [c]A'ishah may God be pleased with her, was a scholar. The least [amount] of poetry she had memorized ... al-Zuhri said: "[c]A'ishah had memorized, by way of poetry, eighteen thousand lines of verse.

## Selection 17

أيضًا وضعُها في عمل لايليق بمكانتها كما أسلفت كرعي الأغنام والخروج للاحتطاب وكذلك تدريبها على السلاح ودخولها في الجيش وفي المرور وفي مواجهة الناس كفي الجوازات وعلى المنافذ العامة وفي المستشفيات لمباشرة الرجال وفي النوادي الطبية وفي أماكن التمريض . كل هذا لايجوز في الإسلام . فلابد أن يكون عملَها أن يكون عملُها في حقلها مع بنات جنسها لاترى الرجال ولايرونها . وقد سألت صحابية رسول الله عليه الصلاة والسلام في حديث حسن << ما أحسن شئ للمرأة ؟ قال ألا ترى الرجال ولايرونها . >>

The same is [true] of putting her in a task which is not suitable to her status, as I mentioned earlier, like herding sheep, going out to gather firewood, and so on -- training her on weapons and going into the army or the traffic police or coming face to face with people as in passport offices or in public access ways or in hospitals tending men or in medical circles or nursing positions. All of this is not permissible in Islam. Her work must ... her work must be in her [proper] field with girls of her own gender not seeing men and they not seeing her. One of the women-companions asked the prophet, may God bless him and grant him peace, in a fine *hadith* : "What is the best thing for woman?" [The Prophet] said: "That she not see men and they not see her."

## Selection 18

مما نعانيه نسبة المشاكل كلها إليها وأنها مصدر الإزعاج وأصبح عند بعض الناس عقدة أن كل مشكلة في البيت من جانب المرأة وتجد حتى في القضايا الشرعية عند القضاة إذا أتى رجل يتحدث بسط لسانه في زوجته وتكلم عن ظلمها وعن سائتها وهي خجولة لا تستطيع أن تبدي حجتها فيظلمها ويزيد عليها حتى يذكر سبحانه وتعالى في الكتاب قال عن المشركين << أو مَن يُنشّأ في الحلية وهو في الخصام غير مبين >> قالوا هي المرأة لاتبين في الخصام ولا تدافع عن نفسها ولا تعرف أن تعرض حجتها فيستغل ذلك كثير من الناس حتى في القضايا الأسرية فإذا أتوا إلى الحكَم من أهلها والحكم من أهله أتى الرجل يتكلم بالمحاضرات لأنه جريئ ويفتعل الأقاويل وأتت هي تبكي خجولة لاتستطيع أن تدافع عن نفسها . فليتقَ الله الناس في هذا ولاينسبوا المشاكل للنساء فإنه لايحدث في البيت الامور إلا وكان للرجل ضلعا في ذلك أو ربما في الحالات النادرة تكون المرأة سبباً رئيسياً لكن ليس دائماً ونريد أن نزيل عقدة نسبة الخطأ دائماً إلى المرأة

Among [the problems] from which we suffer is the association of [our] problems -- all of them -- with [woman] and [our assertion] that she is the source of [our] annoyance. [This] has become, for some people, a psychological complex -- that every problem in the home is on woman's part. You will even find, in *shari$^{c}$ah* cases before judges, when a man comes to speak he excoriates his wife and speaks of her injustice and her evil while she is shy, unable to present her argument. So he unjustly accuses her and overstates [his case] against her such that even [God], may He be glorified and exalted, says, in the Book (He spoke of polytheists): "And what of he who is reared amid jewels but is, at the time of dispute, not to be seen?"* They have said: "It is woman not being clear in argument and who does not defend herself and does not know [how] to present her case [that is the problem]." But, many people exploit that, even in family legal cases. If some of her family or his family are brought before judgement, the man comes along giving lectures because he is daring and does well with words, but she comes along crying, abashed, not being able to defend herself. Then let people fear God in this [situation] and not ascribe problems to women. Things do not happen in the home unless the man has a hand in it. Or, perhaps in rare circumstances the woman is the chief cause but not always. We want to do away with the complex of always ascribing fault to the woman.

* Qur'an 43:18; the "dispute" here is especially legal contention.

## Selection 19

منها عدم فتح مجالات الدعوة للمرأة وسبق كثيرا أن ينادي الدعاة في هذا المكان وفي غيره إلى مراكز الدعوة المحترمة أن تجعل هناك دروس للنساء تقوم امرأة تدرس بنات جنسها أو حلقات تعليمية في القرآن وفي علم الحديث والتفسير والفقه وأن تقوم المرأة كذلك في حيها بجمع جارتها على درس أسبوعي أو في القرى

Among [our problems] is the failure to open proselytizing opportunities for woman. Preachers have often called, previously -- in this place and elsewhere, for respectable proselytizing centers; that lessons there be made available for women. A woman [might] get up and teach others of her gender. Or [we might set up] educational circles on the Qur'an and on the science of *hadith* and exegesis and law. [It might be] that woman might undertake, likewise -- in her neighborhood, to gather her neighbors for a weekly lesson, or [she might do likewise] in the villages.

## Selection 20

وقد وصلني أخ فاضل أكرمه الله من أهل يزيد باقتراح جيد عجيب رائع للمرأة وهو ينص على أن يكون هناك مجموعات من الفتيات يتولين في كل امرأة قريتها إرشاد النساء لأن المرأة تعيش اكتساحا رهيبا لايعلمه إلا الله محاربة ومهددة في عرضها وفي دينها من كل جهة الجمعيات النسائية الفيديوهات الاطروحات الأشرطة المجلات الدوريات التلفاز االدعايات المغرضة ومع ذلك لابد أن نتواصى وأن نتعاون طيب نحن يعني ذهبنا في ... مذهبا جميلا في مسألة المحاضرات والدورس واللقاءت والندوات لرجال لكن مسألة النساء فأنا أضع هذا ولكل منكم أن يقترح اقتراحاً يرضاه ويراه ويشاور أهل

بيته إن كانوا من الداعيات أو طالبات العلم أو الصالحات

A gracious brother, may God bless him -- he's from the people of Yazid, has sent on to me a fine, pleasing, wonderful suggestion for woman. It provides that there be groups of young women taking charge -- each woman having her [own] village -- of guiding women because woman lives in a frightful [situation] of being overwhelmed which only God realizes. [She is] attacked and threatened in her honor and her religion from every direction: women's organizations, videos, public announcements, tapes, magazines, periodicals, television, biased commercials! Despite that, we must counsel [her] and cooperate [with her]. Fine. We, I mean, have gone along a lovely path on the question of lectures and lessons and meetings and gatherings for men. But, [as for] the problem of women, I have laid out this [suggestion]. But, it is up to each of you to make a suggestion which will please [each one of you] and which each one of you will see [as useful] and consult his family if they are preaching women or seekers of knowledge or doers of good deeds

## Selection 21

توجيه الغزو الفكري والخلقي للمرأة بواسطة المجلات والافلام والنشرات والأغاني — رأيت في بعض الأسواق هنا في أبها أكثر من ثمانية عشر مجلة تحمل صورة المرأة على الغلاف صورة المرأة الفاتنة وهم يعرضون المرأة في باب الجمال فقط لا يعرضونها من باب الدين أو أنهم يشيدون بعقلها أو بمكانتها أو بمستواها العلمي أو الثقافي أو بذكائها أو بمصداقيتها أو بطهرها إنما بجانب الجمال المتهتك . وأنا أعتقد اعتقاداً جازماً أن اللواتي خرجن في بالمجلات للبيع قد بعن أنفسهن من قبل هذه الصورفي سوق رخيص هو سوق النخاسة العالمي لضياع المرأة إنّا نعوذ بالله من الفتن

Directing intellectual and moral attack against woman by means of magazines, films, publications, and songs -- I have seen in some markets, here in Abha, more than eighteen magazines having a picture of woman on the cover -- a picture of a seductive woman. They present woman only in the realm of beauty; they do not present her in the realm of religion nor do they celebrate her intelligence, her status, her academic or cultural level, her cleverness, her credibility, or her purity -- only the facet of shameless beauty. I believe firmly that those [women] who have come out [of their homes to display themselves] in magazines for sale [in public] have sold themselves through these pictures in a cheap market, it being the international sex-slave market to the ruination of woman. We seek refuge in God from seduction.

### Selection 22

أيضاً محلات الأزياء تحمل دفاتر كبرى في تفصيلات المودات الجديدة والأشكال والطرازات الحديثة في لباس المرأة وفي زيها وهي تهدد أمن المرأة . أيضاً محلات الخياطة والتفصيل هناك مقاسات كاشفة فاضحة عارية تعرض في البيوت . وبعض الفتيات يرسلن السائق أو ترسل أخاها إذا كان دبشا فيذهب فيأتي بالمجلات ويعرض عليهن المجلة في البيت وغير ذلك من هذه الامور . أيضاً تعرض في محلات بعض محلات ما يسمى « سوبر ماركت » وهو الأسواق الحافلة صور متهتكة ودعايات وهذه منتشرة على العلب وعلى الكراتين وأصبحت عند العالم الكافر المتخلف علامة للدعاية والجذب ليس إلا وتجدونها في بعض الأفلام وفي بعض الدوريات حمانا الله وإياكم

Also, clothing stores carry [the] largest catalogs with details of the new fashions and the new sorts and types of woman's clothes and dress, and they threaten woman's security. Too, [in] sewing and detail stores there are exposing, scandalous, naked patterns which are shown in homes. And, some young women send the chauffeur, or she will send her brother if he is trash. He'll go and come back with the magazines and show the magazine to them in the home and other such sorts of things. Also, there are displayed in stores, some stores -- what are called "Supermarkets," they being lavish markets, shameless pictures and advertisements. They are displayed on cans and cartons. They have become, in the infidel, backward world, the token of advertisement and attraction other than which there is nothing. You [also] find them in some films and in some periodicals, may God protect us and you.

## Selection 23

أيضاً في الأغاني التي أمطرت بها الأسواق وأحرج بها الناس وكما تعرفون الخبر الذي ورد أن أغنية لمغنٍ واحد وصلت إلى الأسواق وبيع منها في أسبوع واحد بخمسين ألف ريال . فقل لي بالله كيف يكون البيت إذا دخل الشريط التسعون دقيقة في البيت وهويحمل خمسة أغاني أو أربعة أغاني كيف يهتك ذاك البيت ويضيعه من أناس لايخافون الله في الجيل ولا في الأمة

Also, [terrible things appear] in songs with which the markets have been inundated and by which people have been embarrassed. As you know, a news item which has come along [states] that a song by one singer reached the markets, and in one week, fifty thousand riyals [worth of copies] of it were sold. So tell me, by God, what will become of a house if this tape, ninety minutes, gets into the house it having five songs or four songs?* How will that house be ripped apart and ruined by people, in this generation or community, who do not fear God?

* Note أغاني for the proper أغانٍ .

## Selection 24

تقديم الأولاد من النقص الذي نعيشه تقديم الأولاد عند الباب على البنات في الحب والتقدير والإكرام -- فتجد بعض الجهلة يقدم ابنائه بالحترام ولو كانت البنت أكبر. فيعطي الفنجال الإبن والبنت أكبر. ويسلم على الإبن قبل ويقدم الإبن في الركوب ويقدمه في أشياء تشعر البنت بإزاءه بالنقص وتشعر بالتقصير وتشعر بالإحتقار وهذا لايقره الإسلام يا إخوتي في الله الواجب العدل << إتقوا الله واعدلوا بين أولادكم >> كما قال عليه الصلاة والسلام

Favoring boys is [part] of the prejudice [in] which we live; favoring boys over girls, from the start, in love, respect and generosity-- You will find some of the ignorant favoring their sons, in [terms of] respect, even if the daughter is older. [Such a person] will give the cup [to] the son [first] while the daughter is older. He will greet the son first and favor the son in giving him a ride. And while [the father] is favoring [the son] in [such] things, the daughter feels, faced with this, inferiority; she feels [that she] falls short; she feels scorn, and Islam does not command this. O my brothers in God [our] just duty is "fear God and deal justly with your children" as [the Prophet], blessings and peace be upon him, said.

## Selection 25

جُعلت المرأة في كثير من الأماكن وسيلة لدعاية وقد مر شئ من ذلك .
ولكن وُضعت مضيفات . وإن من المآسي التي تعيشها الأمة أن تكون
المضيفات في الطائرات نساء ولو أن حجب شعرهن . فإنها مأساة
ليس لها جواب . ولايستطيع أن يجاوب أحد إلا أنها مأساة حتى يقول
أهل الخطوط ونفس كادر الطائرة أو طاقم الطائرة هذه مأساة نعيشها
ليس لها جواب ... ليس لها جواب . أن يركب مائة وخمسين أو مئتان
... أو ... مائتين من الركاب المسلمين المصلين الناسكين فيفاجئون
بأربع مضيفات مختارات جميلات . رأيت في مجلة أو في جريدة
الأهرام قطعة أرسلها بعض الإخوة لي إعلاناً أن شركة الخطوط تريد
مضيفات يعني من بلاد أجنبية . واشترطوا شروطاً أن يكون عمرها
من أربع وعشرين إلى تسعة عشر لاتزيد ولا تنقص وأن تكون جميلة
إلى غير ذلك . فعرفنا أن المقصد مقصداً << يوماً يمان إذا لاقيتُ ذا
يمن وإن لقيتُ معدياً فعدنان >> وكذلك سكرتيرات في بعض المكاتب
وبعض السفارات وبعض المنتديات والنوادي وكذلك في الفنادق
وأماكن تجمّع الناس كالمستشفيات والعيادات وأماكن التمريض وهذا
من احتقار المرأة ومن تبذلها ومن عرضها للشرهاء والفجرة

Woman has been made, in many places, into an instrument of propaganda, and some [reference] to that [has already been] gone over. But, they have been placed [as] stewardesses. Certainly, among the crises which the community is experiencing is [the fact] that stewardesses on airplanes are women, even if their hair is covered. It is a crisis that has no answer. No one can answer [by saying anything] but that it is a crisis. Even the airline people, and even the airplane cadre or air crews, say: "this is a crisis through which we are living." It has no answer. That two hundred fifty or two hundred ... or ... two hundred pious, praying, Muslim passengers are stunned by four selected, beautiful stewardesses.... I saw -- in a magazine ... or [rather] in the *Ahram* newspaper -- a piece, which some of the brothers sent to me, an advertisement that an airline company was wanting some stewardesses, I mean from a foreign country. And, they set out conditions that their age be from twenty-four to nineteen, and no more and no less, and that they be pretty, and so on. So, we knew that the intention was clear: "Oh what a day should I meet Dha Yemen, and if I meet a Ma$^{c}$addite, [I know that] he is [of the tribe of] $^{C}$Adnan."* The same [is true for] secretaries in some offices and some embassies and some clubs and societies. The same [is true] in some hotels and places where people gather, and hospitals and clinics and in nursing situations. This is scorn for woman; this is her being vulgar, and [this is] exposing her to the greedy and the shamless.

* I have been unable to trace this line of بسيط meter poetry and find the first hemistich uncertain and obscure out of its particular context. The second hemistich, and the context of Sheikh Safar's comments, makes its general intent clear enough, however. We recognize the sexually immoral intent of the airline company even though it is not explicit as we recognize a member of the Ma$^{C}$add clan as being of the $^{C}$Adnan tribe.

## Selection 26

ومنها أن الكثير من الناس يدعون إلى التعدد ولا يذكرون العدل بين الزوجات الذي هو الأهم فإن كثير من المحاضرين والدعاة يدعوا الناس إلى أن يعددوا وأن يكثروا من الزوجات بينما لم يذكر في محاضرة واحدة العدل بين الزوجات فإن هذا أهم وإذا حُلّ مسألة العدل ارتاح الناس وكانت مسألة التعدد سهلة لكن أن يتحدث عن هذا وأن يدعوا الناس و ينشّط الناس للتعدد ثم يترك المشكلة الكبرى وهي عدم العدل فهذا خاطئ ولذلك وُجد من تزوج مثلاً بثانية فأهمل الأولى تماماً وجعلها ليست مطلقة ولا متزوّجة وإنما هي معلقة وجعلها كأنها خُلقت هكذا صفراً على الشمال ليس لها اعتبارفي الحياة وهذا من الخطأ ومنهم من ظلم حتى إنه يعطي هذه ثلاث ليالي وهذه ليلة ومنهم من لا يعدل في النفقة ولا في الخلق ولا في السكنى ولا في الإطعام ولا في غير ذلك مما يجب العدل فيه

And among [these crises] is [the fact] that many people call for polygamy but do not mention justice between wives which is most important. Many speakers and preachers call people to polygamy and to multiplying [the number of their] wives while "justice among wives" is not mentioned in a single lecture. But the latter is the more important. If the problem of "justice" were solved, people would be content, and the problem of polygamy would be simple, but that [anyone] should speak about this [matter] and encourage people and stir them up about polygamy and then leave aside the greatest problem -- the lack of justice -- that is mistaken. For that reason he who has married, for example, a second wife is to be found, but he ignores the first [wife] completely. He has put her in the position of being neither divorced nor married. She is, rather, "suspended." He has put her in the position of being made a "zero to the left."* She has no consideration in life, and this is wrong. And, among them are those who have done wrong to the extent that he gives this [wife] three nights and that [wife] a single night. And, there are those who do not do justice in expenditures, nor in morals, nor in housing, nor in food, nor in other things in which justice should be [done].

* Zero to the left" -- of the decimal point; i.e. less than whole, without value especially intellectually.

## Selection 27

أيضاً منها النقص الذي نعيشه مطالبة المرأة بحقوق الرجل دون ذكر حقوق المرأة عند الرجل . تجد كثيراً من الناس يطلبون من المرأة أن تؤدي حقوق الرجل . وكثرت الأشرطة والمحاضرات والندوات في حق الرجل على المرأة . دائماً حق الرجل على المرأة لكننا نحتاج إلى حق المرأة على الرجل . ونحن مثلنا في هذا مثل الشعوب المستضعفة . فإن الشعوب الان دائماً يقولون عليكم بالطاعة للقادة والقائمين . وعليكم أن تتقوا الله . وعليكم بالمحافظة . لكن حقوق هؤلاء الشعوب ما تُذكر. تجد الشعوب أما مهضومة أو مظلومة أو محتقرة أو جائعة أو ترمى على الأرصفة أو لا مكان لها أو لا رأي أو لا احترام أو لا مشاركة أو لا تقدير. ومع ذلك وسائل الإعلام صباح مساء إتقوا الله وأدوا حقوق الولاة والزعماء فإنكم إن لم تفعلوا خرجتم من الملة وخرجتم من الدين . فمثل هذا مثل ذاك . المرأة الان مثل الدول النامية النائمة . نعم مثل التعامل معها كذلك التعامل معها بعنف وفظاظة إلى درجة الضرب لغير إذن شرعي حتى إن بعضهم يعلق مشعاباً في البيت مهمته زوجته ويسمى المشعاب ستر الله وهذا المشعاب ليس بسترالله لكنه يغضب الله أحياناً لغير إذن شرعي وقد قال صلى الله عليه وسلم في الصحيح لقد طاف بأبيات آل محمد أناس يضربون ... لقد طاف بأبيات آل محمد نساء يشتكين من أزواجهن

وإن اولئك ليسوا بأخياركم أو من خيرتكم أو كما قال صلى الله عليه
وسلم الحديث صحيح النساء شكين عليه صلى الله عليه وسلم يطفن
على نسائه يشكين من بعض الرجال يضربن يضرب واحد إمراته ضرباً
مبرحاً فمن يفعل ذلك ليس من خيرة الناس

Also among [these crises] -- the shortfall which we are living through -- is woman's demand for the rights *of* man without any mention of woman's right *from* man. You will find many people demanding of woman that she take up the rights of man, and tapes, lectures, and meetings about man's rights *over* woman are plentiful: always "man's rights *over* woman." But, we need "woman's right over man." And, we, [and] the likes of us, in this [regard] are like oppressed peoples. As for the peoples now, [others] are always saying: "You must be obedient to leaders and rulers. You must fear God; you must be conservative!" But those peoples' rights are not mentioned. You find people to be either terrorized, unjustly treated, scorned, starving or thrown [out] on the sidewalks or without a place; without an opinion, without respect, without participation or regard. And despite that, the news media, morning and evening [say]: "Fear God and render to the state and leaders [their] rights. And, if you don't do so, you are expelled from the community, and you are expelled from the religion. And, as is the one so is the other. Woman, now, is like the sleeping, developing countries. Yes! As she is dealt with, so are they dealt with -- with violence and force to the extent of beatings without lawful permission. So much so that some of [these people] hang a switch u[p outside] the house the target of which is his wife. And the switch is called "God's protection." But, this switch is not "God's protection," but sometimes it angers God because there is no lawful permission [for that]. And, [the Prophet], may God bless him and grant him peace, said, in the *Sahih,* "People striking out walked around the homes of Muhammad's family.... Women complaining about their husbands walked around the homes of Muhammad's family, and indeed those are not your best or the best of you." [It is] as he, may God bless him and grant him peace, said. The *hadith* is true: the women complained to him, may God bless him and grant him peace, walking around his women complaining of some of the men striking out [at them]. A certain one strikes his wife in a way causing pain; whoever does that is not among the best of people.

## Selection 28

وتجد كذلك كثير من الشبيبة سّمار. يسمرون في المقاهي من الموظفين وأمثالهم يأخذ ينطلق الواحد منهم بعد صلاة العشاء ويغلق على امرأته في بيته لا هو أطعمها وسقاها ولا هو تركها تأكل من خشاش الأرض فيذهب يسمر إلى الثانيه عشرة ليلاً أو الواحدة ثم يدخل عليها في آخر الليل وهو منهك ويلقي نفسه على الفراش. طيب من يتحدث معها ؟ ومن يمزح معها ؟ من يلاطفها ؟ من يعطيها الأخبار ؟ وقد أتت شكايات ورسائل من هذا الصنف كثيروكثير. وبعضهن تطلب الفراق. تقول أنا مع أمي في بيتي أحسن من مصاحبة هذا. ما أراه إلا نائماً أو غريباً بعيداً وغير ذلك وبعضهم مضياف تجد بيته دائماً يستقبل في كل وقت ويترك إمرأته فقد يجعلها آمرة ... مأمورة دائماً منهية. يأخذ الشاهي والبخور والقهوة والطعام وغير ذلك أما امرأته فما كسبت وقتاً من وقت الأضياف الذين أخذوا عمره عليه. ولا أدعو إلى البخل لكن دين الله وسط. للضيف وقت إن لأهلك عليك حقاً ولضيفك عليك حقاً

And, you will find many of the youth partying, staying out late in the coffee shops -- some of them state employees and their like -- taking .... one of them takes off after the evening prayer. He locks his wife in his house without having given her anything to eat, without having given her anything to drink, without even having left her any grass from the lawn to eat. And, he goes off to party until twelve at night, or one, and then, he goes in to her at the end of the night, he being exhausted, and throws himself on the bed. OK! Who is to speak with her? Who is to joke with her? Who is to treat her kindly? Who is to give her the news? Complaints and letters of this kind have come in very often. Some [such women] ask for separation; they say: "I, being with my mother in my [family's] home, am better [off] than in the company of this [person] whom I only see when he's sleeping or [behaving] strangely, distant or something else of that [sort]. Some of [these husbands] are hospitable. You'll always find him at home receiving [guests] at every hour [of the day or night]. He leaves his wife. He makes her [take] orders ... under orders, always finished with. He takes tea, and incense, and coffee, and food and so on. But as for his wife, she gains nothing of the time [allotted] to the guests who have taken his whole life from him. I'm not calling for miserliness, but God's religion is moderate. There is a [proper] time for the guest. Indeed you owe your family a certain duty, and you owe your guest a certain duty.

## Selection 29

التجريح عند البعض من النساء بكلمات محرقة كاللعن — والعياذ بالله — آخرها امرأة في عصرهذا اليوم اتصلت تبكي تقول لعنها زوجها أكثر من جبال ما أدري ايش . نعوذ بالله . ويدل على قلة دينه وعلى قلة خوفه . أسأل الله أن يصلحه . وكثير منهن تتوهم أن اللعنة طلاق وأنها تنفذ وتخرج من عصمته . والصحيح أنه لا . اللعنة كبيرة من الكبائر. عليه أن يتوب وأن يستغفر لكن ما يكتب بها طلقة. وإن يحذر الأزواج ألا يستخدموا اللعن ولا الشتم بل بعضهم والعياذ بالله يقذف زوجته فإذا غضب عليها قذفها في عرضها قذفا لو وصلت إلى المحكمة لأقيم عليه الحد عليه حد القاذف . وبعضهم يسبها ويسب أهلهاو والديها ويلعن والديها أو يلعن قبيلتها أو يلعن أسرتها والعياذ بالله . وهذا من الجهل ومن قلة مراقبة الله . فاتقوا الله في دلك . إمساك بمعروف أو تسريح بإحسان أحد الأمرين . إن أحببتها فأمسكها محترمة وإلا — إن لم تحبها وليس لها في قلبك منزلة — فخذها بكل احترام واوصلها إلى أهلها

Some [men's] wounding of women by burning words, like cursing -- all protection is [only] in God -- The latest [example] of it is a woman, this afternoon, who contacted [me] crying, saying her husband had cursed her more than the mountains. I don't know what.* We seek protection in God. It indicates the paucity of his religion and the paucity of his fear [of God]. I beg God that He reform him. Many of [these women] imagine that this cursing is [equivalent] to divorce and that she has been dismissed and is cast out of the bond [of marriage .] The truth is that it is not so. Cursing is a very great [sin]. [The husband] should repent and seek [God's] forgiveness, but divorce is not decreed by [a curse]. Husbands [should be] warned not to use the curse nor the insult, but some of them, and refuge is to be found in God, slander [their] wife. If he gets angry with her, [if] he slanders her honor seriously, [and] if [the case] goes to court, then the penalty will be applied to him, the penalty for a slanderer. Some of them revile her and revile her family and her parents and curse her parents or curse her tribe or curse her family; refuge is to be found in God. This is out of ignorance and out of a paucity of observing God['s law]. So, fear God in this [regard]. Holding fast to what is good or letting free with good will -- one of the two. If you love her, hold fast to her in respect, and if not -- if you don't love her -- and she has no place in your heart, then take her with all respect and send her to her family.

* Note the dialectal forms.

Chapter Four

# Tolerance

## Introduction

"Tolerance" is a concept to which contemporary Western society pays great homage. Whether it be towards others' religious beliefs and practices or towards ideas, behavior or personal status, we tend to privilege "tolerance" (and its assumed concomitant, "respect for human [or individual] rights") above most other values. Westerners also express great concern for what we see as a lack of concern with human rights in Islam and for Muslims' *intolerance*. Such views are so common that they need not be documented at length; a couple of examples will suffice. One is a favorite example of this so common discourse; the second is chosen especially for its timeliness and immediate pertinence.

Mortimer B. Zuckerman, then editor-in-chief of *U.S. News and World Report*, in an editorial of March 22, 1993 entitled "Beware of Religious Stalinists" says:

> The seven leaders of the Muslim Brotherhood ... seemed reasonable at first. Then we heard their message. Their holy obligation, they told us, is to recover all the land once under Muslim rule. The only solution to the Palestinian problem is to destroy Israel through *jihad*, a holy war. Why not then, they were asked, go further afield -- to Spain and to India where Muslim rule once prevailed? "One step at a time," they responded.... We were face to face with the fanaticism that seems the polar opposite of the Western ideal's sanctity for individual life.

On January 24, 1996, National Public Radio's "Morning Edition" reported that the "Christian Coalition" has asked the U.S. State Department to help protect Christians in China, Iran and Saudi Arabia where the practice of Christianity is being suppressed. Indeed , as the associated press noted in September of 1994, "The annual State Department report on worldwide human rights conditions routinely calls attention to alleged abuses in Saudi Arabia."

Sheikh Safar al-Hawli's lecture حكم الاحتفال بأعياد الكفار , "A Condemnation of Celebrating Unbelievers' Holidays," will do little to relieve civil libertarians' concerns about the attitudes of Saudi Arabia's conservative Sheikhs. Indeed the severity of his language and the apparent triviality of the points which seem most to concern him are, respectively, disturbing or laughable at first glance. Three points must, however, be kept well in mind as we examine Sheikh Safar's comments.

The first point we must keep in mind, as we approach Sheikh Safar's lecture, is that our own claims to tolerance are deeply suspect. Despite the gains of the ecumenical movement, many Christians remain deeply intolerant of other religious traditions. A Christian Fundamentalist newsletter reports as follows on 5/22/93 (quotes as in original):

> During her health care travels, First Lady Hillary Rodham Clinton met with American Indian spiritual healers in Montana. Before meeting with them she was "blessed" by an Indian shaman.... New Age occult forces continue to influence the Clinton White House.

The very concept of tolerance is openly excoriated by some Christian commentators. Robert Moynihan of the Catholic World Report puts it this way in a recent fund-raising letter:

> With Communism all but vanquished, Catholicism remains threatened by an even more formidable enemy: Western liberal culture. Today's battle, however, is not against outward and brutal persecution, but against a subtly lethal spirit of "tolerance" that offers Catholics acceptance on condition that we admit that ours is not the One True Faith, but only one faith among many. Such a condition, if accepted, would render Christianity as empty as if its churches were razed, its books burned and its adherents executed.

From the point of view of the religious, secular claims to tolerance also ring hollow. As Stephan Carter shows on page three of his *Culture of Disbelief*, "we have created a political and legal culture that presses the religiously faithful to be other than themselves, to act publicly, and sometimes privately as well, as though their faith does not matter to them." He goes on to press the assertion that:

> Tolerance (of religiosity in a secular nation as well of one religion by another) without respect means little; if I tolerate you but do not respect you, the message of my tolerance, day after day, is that it is my forbearance,

> not your right, and certainly not the nation's commitment to equality, that frees you to practice your religion. You do it by my sufferance, but not with my approval. And since, I merely tolerate, but neither respect nor approve, I might at any time kick away the props, and bring the puny structure of your freedom down around your ears." (p. 93)

In the United States, the higher courts continue, for the most part, to defend religious practices unpopular to secular or mainstream, Christian majorities. The Minnesota state government required the Amish to affix orange, slow-moving-vehicle signs to their black, horse-drawn carriages. The Amish objected on religious grounds and were upheld by the state supreme court. Similarly, Florida banned the ritual sacrifice of animals required by Santeria, an Afro-Cuban religion. The Supreme Court has overturned the ban.

On the other hand, the Supreme Court has allowed an Oregon ruling against a Native American's use of peyote in tribal religious ritual to stand. And for Muslims especially, the tolerance of the Western secular democracies is suspect. In Minneapolis, according to *USA Today* (Oct, 5 1994), police ticketed a veiled Muslim woman citing a little used law that prevents people from hiding their identity "by means of a robe, mask, or other disguise." "'We're angry,' says Magda Saikali, an activist who organized protests over Amatullah's treatment. 'We are harassed all the time because of our clothes .... But this is really too much.'"

On a broader plane, British Secretary of State for Education John Patten called for more national monies for church schools in 1994. As the *Middle East* reported in February of that year, "Muslims campaigning for state support for Muslim schools in Britain found a bitter irony in this since their application for voluntary-aided status for the Islamic primary school in the London borough of Brent had only weeks previously been rejected."

The second point that we must keep in mind is that most Muslims feel strongly that *their's* is, in fact, the religion of tolerance *par excellence*. They cite as proof such Quran'ic verses as "Every nation has its messenger" (10:47) and "Surely they that believe -- the Jews and Christians and Sabians who believe in God and the Last Day and work righteousness -- their wage awaits them with their Lord and no fear shall be on them neither shall they sorrow" (2:58; 5:69). As Cyril Glasse has pointed out, in the article "Ahl al-Kitab" in his *Concise Encyclopedia of Islam*, , "The fact that one Revelation should name others as authentic is an extraordinary event in the history of religions." Muslims also point to Islamic history as testimony, by and large accepted by Western scholars, to the actual religious tolerance of Muslims down through the centuries.

Middle Eastern Christians often concur. Caryle Murphy quotes an Egyptian Christian shoeshine man in his April 26, 1992 *Washington Post* article "The Christian-Muslim Relationship: as Tolerance Erodes, Churches Fear Outcome of Extremism":

> Imbaba used to be a calm place. The original Muslims ... were very educated, understanding, good people..., but after 1968 some of these people arrived (from rural areas). Their brains were infected with this idea of religious extremism .... They are people ignorant of true Islam.

Our third caveat is this: Sheikh Safar does go to the point of hoping to suppress Christian activities entirely and of asserting that Islam does not require, at least, "tolerance of," if not "respect for," the "People of the Book" until Judgement Day. It is to be noted, however, that Sheikh Safar's primary focus is the prevention of Muslims participating in (and in some cases being virtually compelled to participate in) Christian holiday celebrations. That he should urge Muslims not to participate in such activities, since they conflict with their proper religious commitments, is unremarkable if not ecumenical. To the extent that it is true that Muslims are being pressured to take part in Christian practices in Saudi Arabia (in the context of corporate holiday celebrations) one might see Sheikh Safar as a civil libertarian himself.

# Chapter Four

**"Wherein 'Tolerance'?"** from ***A Condemnation of Celebrating Unbelievers' Holidays*** by **Safar al-Hawali**

## Selection 1

أيها الاخوة المؤمنون لا ريب أن لكل قول داعيا وموجبا . وهذا القول أو هذه المحاضرة موجبها وداعيها في هذه الايام أو في هذه الليلة هو أنه كما تعلمون بعد ما يقارب الشهر تقريبا سوف يكون عيد بل عيدان من أعياد المشركين من أعياد الكفار . فقد عهدنا أن الكفار يقيمون أعيادهم في الشركات والمؤسسات والادارات والمجمّعات السكنية علانية أو بما يشبه العلانية . كما عهدنا أن من المسلمين مَن يشاركهم في ذلك ويحضر ويشهد هذا الزور العظيم وتَبدر منهم أفعال لا تليق بمن يعرف الله ورسوله ومن هداه الله تبارك وتعالى للصراط المستقيم وأمره بمخالفة المغضوب عليهم والضالين ومجانبة طريق اصحاب الجحيم . فلذلك أردنا أيها الاخوة في الله أن نجعل هذه المحاضرة إعذاراً إلى الله تبارك وتعالى وإبلاغا لكم ولكل من تبلغه وإنذارا لأولئك الذين قد يفعلون هذا المنكر إما لأنهم كفار لم يلتزموا بما امر الله تبارك وتعالى به ولاسيما في بلا د الاسلام وإما لانهم في غفلة فليتعلموا وليعرفوا حكم الله تبارك وتعالى وليُذكّروا بالله وبما شرع الله تعالى في مثل هذا وإما لأنهم معاندون كما قد يبدر من بعض المنتسبين إلى الاسلام فيعاندون ويصرون على إقامة هذا المنكر بين ظهرانينا ففي هذا الكلام قبل أن يأتي ذلك الموسم إنذار لهم باننا لن نسكت ولن ندع هذا المنكر يمر أبدا

O you believing brothers, there is no doubt that every statement has a cause and a motive. And, this statement, or this "lecture," its motive and cause are, during these days -- on this night .... as you know, in just about a month, there will be a holiday -- or rather two holidays -- among the unbelievers' holidays -- the holidays of the polytheists. We have gotten used to [the idea] that the unbelievers will celebrate their holidays -- at companies, institutions, bureaus and in residential buildings -- publicly or in what amounts to being public. We have also gotten used to [the idea] that there are those Muslims who will participate in these [celebrations]. [Some] will attend and witness this serious falsehood. Acts [may] escape from [those Muslims] which are not suitable for he who knows God and His Messenger; for he whom God, may He be blessed and exalted, has guided toward the "Straight Path" and ordered to oppose "those with whom God is angered and those who go astray" and to avoid the "path of the people of hell fire." Therefore, O brothers in God, we wanted to make this lecture an apology to God, may He be blessed and exalted; an announcement to you, and all those whom it reaches, and a warning to those who may do this evil -- either because they are unbelievers who have not committed themselves to that which God, may He be blessed and exalted, has commanded (and especially in land of Islam) or because they are not aware of it. Let them learn, and let them know the judgement of God, may He be blessed and exalted. Let them be reminded of God and that which God, may He be exalted, has decreed about the like of this. [They may celebrate the unbelievers' holidays] either because they are stubborn, as may happen with some of those affiliated with Islam such that they act stubbornly and insist on doing this kind of sin among us. In this statement, before the season starts, [there] is a warning to them that we will never keep quiet, and we will not let this kind of crime pass, ever.

## Selection 2

إخوتي الكرام عندما نقولأو نتحدث عن حكم الاحتفال بأعياد الكفار فإن من أول ما ينبغي أن نعرفه ما معنى العيد . وذكر شيخ الاسلام ابن تيمية ابن تيمية رحمه الله تعالى في كتابه العظيم وهو كتاب اقتضاء الصراط المستقيم لمخالفة أصحاب الجحيم ذكر هذا وذكر أحكاما أخرى عظيمة نورد بعضا منها إن شاء الله تعالى وقبل ذلك نوصي كل اخ منكم بإقتناء هذا الكتاب القيم النفيس ولاسيما ما حققه اخونا الفاضل الدكتور ناصر العقل حفظه الله وهي موجودة متداولة . و كذلك تراجعون ما ذكره وسطره الامام ابن القيم رحمه الله تعالى في كتابه أحكام أهل الذمة

My honorable brothers, when we speak, or talk, about the "condemnation of celebrating unbelievers' holidays," one of the first things which we should know is the meaning of "holiday." The Sheikh al-Islam, Ibn Taymiyyah -- Ibn Taymiyyah, may God have mercy on him, mentioned, in his great book (its title being: *The Straight Path's Requirement to Oppose the People of Hellfire*), he mentioned this [matter of the unbelievers' holidays] and other great rulings some of which we will bring forward God, may He be exalted, willing. Before that, I would advise every brother among you to acquire this valuable, precious book, especially that [edition] which our gracious brother, Dr. Naser al-$^{C}$Aql (may God preserve him), has edited, it being available and in circulation. You should also refer that which Imam Ibn al-Qayyim [al-Jawziyyah], may God (exalted be He) have mercy on him, said and wrote down in his book, *Rulings on the Ahl al-Dhimmah.*

## Selection 3

أقول إن شيخ الاسلام رحمه الله عرّف العيد فقال العيد اسم جنس
يدخل فيه كل يوم او مكان لهم -- أي للكفار أو لأي أحد -- فيه اجتماع
-- لهم فيه اجتماع -- وكل عمل يحدثونه في هذه الامكنة والازمنة

I say: the Sheikh al-Islam, may God have mercy on him, has defined "holiday." He said: "It is a generic noun under which is included every day or place of theirs ..." (that is 'of the unbelievers' or of anyone [else]) "...in which [there] is a meeting, ..." (they have a meeting in it) "...and every action they perform in these places and times."

## Selection 4

ويقول << أعياد الكفار كثيرة>> وهذه حقيقة ونحن الان في هذا البلد
نرى الكفار كثيرين ومن أديان شتى فلنعلم أنه كما قال رحمه الله
<< أعياد الكفار كثيرة و مختلفة وليس على المسلم أن يبحث عنها ولا
أن يعرفها بل يكفيه أن يعرف في أي فعل من الافعال في أي يوم من
الايام في أي مكان من الامكنة ويجتنب ذلك .>>

And, [Ibn Taymiyyah] says: "The unbelievers' holidays are many." This is true. And, we, now -- in this country, see unbelievers -- many [of them] and of all kinds of religions. So, let us realize that, as [Ibn Taymiyyah], may God have mercy on him, said: "The holidays of the unbelievers are many and various, and the Muslim should not search them out or know [anything of] them. Rather, it is enough for him to know of any [such] activity, of any [such] day, of any [such] place and avoid it."

## Selection 5

وعلى المسلم أن يعرف أماكنها إن كانت مكانية أو أزمنتها إن كانت زمانية فيتجنب ذلك ويتجنب ما نهى عنه النبي صلى الله عليه وسلم من أمور سوف نفصلها بأدلتها إن شاء الله تبارك وتعالى .

The Muslim must know [such holidays'] locations if they are locational or their times if they are temporal so he might avoid th[em] and avoid those matters which the Prophet (may God bless him and grant him peace) has prohibited which we will detail, with evidences about them, God (may He be blessed and exalted) willing.

## Selection 6

وقد ذهب بعض العلماء إلى أنه تنبغي مخالفتهم أو أخذ من الاوامر بمخالفتهم وسنعرض لها إن شاء الله قال يجب أن يخالفوا ومن ذلك أنهم قالوا تصام هذه الايام -- أن يصوم المسلم يوم العيد الذي يحتفل به الكفار . فمن نظر إلى أصل المخالفة وأنها مشروعة قال من مخالفتهم أن يكونوا فرحين مبتهجين يأكلون ويشربون ويعربدون يفعلون ما لا -- كما هو معلوم -- ما لا قد يذكر لا يجوز ذكره قال وهو يكون صائما لله تبارك وتعالى فيكون قد حقق المخالفة . وقال بعض العلماء إلا ... لا يصام يوم من أيام أعيادهم وذلك خشية الوقوع في التعظيم إذ قد يظن ظانّ أنه إنما صيم لانه يوم معظم فكأن هذا يعظمه بالاحتفال والاكل والشرب وذاك يعظمه بصيامه والتقرب إلى الله فيه. وهذا هو الاظهر هذا هو الاظهر والارجح أن المؤمن في هذا اليوم لا يتعمد فعل أي شئ مطلقا وإنما كل حياته أو كل أموره تكون كسائر الايام ويعمل كل عمل كان يعمله في بقية الايام ولا يعبأ ولا يلتفت إلى هذا .

Some scholars go so far as to say that [the unbelievers] ought to be opposed or to issue orders to oppose them. We will turn to that, God willing. [Ibn Taymiyyah] said: "They must be opposed," and therefore, [other scholars] have said: "These days are to be fasted [upon]" -- that Muslims should fast during the holiday which the unbelievers celebrate. He who has looked into the origin of this infraction even, though it is legal, has said: "a part[ial way] of opposing them is that they be happy, joyful, eating, drinking, playing and doing -- as is well known -- things which may not be mentioned, the mention of which is not permissible, [as he] said, while [the Muslim] is fasting before God, may He be blessed and exalted." Thus, [the Muslim] will have implemented [his] opposition. Some scholars have said: "No! None of their holidays should be fasted [upon]" that being out of fear of falling into the glorification [of the holiday] since someone might imagine that [the holiday] is being fasting [upon] because it is a sanctified day. It would be as if the former [the unbeliever] were sanctifying it by celebrating, eating, and drinking, while the latter [the Muslim] were sanctifying it by fasting [on] it and drawing closer to God during it. This is most apparent; this is most apparent and preferable -- that the believer, on such a day, not agree to do anything [special]. Rather, all his life or all his affairs [ought] to be like every other day. He ought to do every act which he would [usually] do on other days and not pay any attention, nor take heed of, [the holiday].

## Selection 7

والكفار أيها الاخوة الكرام الذين بيّن الله تبارك وتعالى لنا عداوتهم في آيٍ كثيرة جدا « إن الكافرين كانوا لكم عدواً مبينا » و كما قال تبارك وتعالى « ياأيها الذين آمنوا لا تتخذوا عدوي وعدوكم أولياء » وكما قال « ياأيها الذين آمنوا لا تتخذوا اليهود والنصارى أولياء» وكذلك بيّن الله تبارك وتعالى وسماهم حزب الشيطان واولياءه وأولياء الطاغوت إلى غير ذلك هؤلاء مجموع الادلة التي جاءت في الكتاب والسنة يمكن أن تصنفهم بحسب مشابهتهم في أعيادهم وغيرها إلى قسمين القسم الاول هم أهل الكتاب اليهودوالنصارى والقسم الثاني الاعاجم وهذا نستطيع أن نأخذه من قول النبي صلى الله عليه وسلم « لتتبعنّ أو لتركبنّ سنن من كان قبلكم حذو القذة بالقذة حتى لودخلوا جفرة ضب لدخلتموه»

The unbelievers, O honored brothers, are those whose enmity towards us God, may He be blessed and exalted, has made clear in very many verses: "The unbelievers are truly open enemies to you."* And, as God, may He be blessed and exalted, said: "O you who believe! Do not take My enemy and yours as friends."† And, as He said: "O you who believe! Take not the Jews and the Christians as friends."‡ Likewise, God, may He be blessed and exalted, has clarified [things] and has named [unbelievers] "the party of the Devil and his friends" and "friends of the Tempter" and so on. These are a collection of proofs which have come from "The Book" and the *Sunnah*; you can categorize them, according to the similarity of their holidays, in two groups. The first group is the "People of the Book," the Jews and the Christians; the second group is the non-Arabs. We can take this from the saying of the Prophet, may God bless him and grant him peace: "You will certainly follow or pursue the paths of those who were before you so perfectly that were they to enter even a lizard's hole you would enter it [too]."

* Quran 4:101.
† Qur'an 40:1.
‡ Qur'an 5:51.

## Selection 8

إن مشاركة أهل الكتاب في أعيادهم أشد نهيا وأشد ضررا وأقل ما يقال إنهما سواء.

Joining the People of the Book in their holidays is more strongly prohibited and more harmful [than participating in other, non-religious, kinds of holidays]. The least that can be said is that they are equal.

## Selection 9

فلا يقولنّ أحد من الناس إن المقصود هم المشركون فقط وأما أهل الكتاب فإن بيننا وبينهم من الاحكام ما لا يدخل فيه غيرهم كما قد يظن وقد نص شيخ الاسلام رحمه الله تعالى على عيد الميلاد بالذات كما قال .... فقال « وكذلك أعياد الفرس مثل النيروز والمهرجان وأعياد اليهود أو غيرهم من أنواع الكفار أوالاعاجم أو الاعراب . »

So, no one says that the intended [reference] was the Polytheists only, [no one should say:] "but as for the people of the Book, there are between us [Muslims] and them [similar] injunctions into which others than they do not come as might be thought." The Sheikh al-Islam, may God (be He exalted) have mercy on him, made reference Christmas in particular. He also said ... ahh .... He said: "Likewise [forbidden] are the Persians' holidays, such as Nairuz and Mihrajan, and the Jews' holidays or other types of unbelievers or non-Arabs or Bedouins."

## Selection 10

من أعياد اليهود عيد الغفران كما يسمونه وكثير منها ما تزال
معاصرة يعني بهذه المناسبة يا إخوان أعياد الكفار محدثة بدعية
ولذلك تجدون أن النصارى في بلاد الشام ومصر في القديم لهم أعياد
واسماء تخالف في بعض منها الموجود لديهم الآن وكذلك في الايام
وأحيانا أيضا في الاسماء يختلف نصارى المشرق مع نصارى المغرب
واليهود القدماء أيضا مع اليهود المتأخرين وما سبب ذلك إلا الابتداع
لان لكل مبتدع فاذا فُتح باب الابتداع ابتدع كل ما شاء وضع ما يشاء
فمجامعهم الكنسية المقدسة كما يزعمون تبتدع أعيادا وتضع من
عندها فقد يشتبه الامر قد تختلف الاسماء ولكن المهم هو أنها إن
حكمها واحد فيقول شيخ الاسلام في هذا قال وكما قال مثل النيروز
والمهرجان وغيرها قال «حكمها كلها هو واحد» قال «وكما لا نتشبه
بِهم في الاعياد فلا يستعان ... فلا يعان المسلم المتشبه بهم في ذلك بل
يُنهى عن ذلك .»

Among the Jews' holidays is Yom-Kippur, as they call it. And, many of [their holidays] are still current. I mean, in this connection -- O brothers, the unbelievers holidays are recently created, heretical. Therefore, you will find that the Christians in Syria and Egypt, in the past, had holidays and names [of holidays] which are different from some of the current ones they now have. Similarly, as to dates and sometimes also names, the Christians of the East differ with the Christians of the West. The ancient Jews also [differ] with later Jews. The reason for that is nothing but heretical innovation because everything is [the result of] innovation. If the gate of heresy is opened, everyone commits heresy as much as he likes and produces whatever he wants to. Their clerical organizations, "holy" as they claim, create holidays and set out [changes] by themselves. The matter has become suspicious. The names might differ, but the important [thing] is that ... that the condemnation of it is one [and the same]. The Sheikh al-Islam says about this ... He said: "... and as ..." He said: " ... such as Nairuz and Mihrajan and others ...." He said: "The condemnation of them, all, is one [and the same]." He said: "As we do not imitate them as regards holidays, the Muslim imitating them in that regard is not sought out for help ... is not aided, rather he is forbidden from [imitating them].

## Selection 11

وذكر الكاتبون في الملل والاديان — ولا مجال الان لصد ذلك — أن عيد الميلاد الذي يحتفل به هؤلاء النصارى اليوم — وهو اكثر ما يضايقنا من الاعياد في هذه البلاد — أنه عيد وثني قديم ثم لما اتخذ النصارى واتبعوا طرائق المجوس وغيرهم من الامم — كما فعل بولس الذي أفسد دينهم وكان على دين المثرائية وبعض الفلسفات الشرقية — نقلوا هذا العيد الوثني القديم وجعلوه من أعيادهم . فهو في الحقيقة لا أصل له في دينهم هم فضلا عن أن يكون له أصل في ديننا

Authors on communities and religions have mentioned --though there is no room now to deal with this -- that the Christmas holiday which those Christians celebrate today -- it being the one of all the holidays which most annoys us in this country -- is an ancient pagan holiday. Then, when the Christians began to follow the traditions of the Magians and of other communities (as did Paul who corrupted their religion, he having been [a follower] of the religion of Mithra'ism and other Eastern philosophies), they brought this ancient pagan holiday and made it one of their holidays. In fact, it does not have any basis in their religion, let alone having any basis in our religion.

## Selection 12

وهي — إذا كان ما يستعان به ... ما قد يستعين به بعض المسلمين على مشابهة الكفار أو الاحتفال بعيدهم — يحرم أن يباع لهم وهو من الطعام أو اللباس أو ما اشبه ذلك فما بالكم ببيع الكروت أو البطاقات التي هي للتهنئة بهذا العيد فمابالكم بمن يشارك أو يدخل أو يندمج في هذا العيد ويحضر ويشهد هذا الزور

And, "it" (even if "it" is that from which justification is sought ... that which some Muslims might use to justify imitating the unbelievers or celebrating their holidays)* is forbidden to be sold to them --"it" being food, clothing or whatever is similar to this. What, then, do you think about selling Christmas cards or the notes which serve to give greetings on this holiday? What do you think about someone who participates in, or gets into or mixes in, this holiday and attends and witnesses this sin?!

* I.e. some Muslims justify themselves (lit. "seek assistance") in attending these holidays by asserting that they are just engaging in commerce. Ibn Taymiyyah condemns even the sale of food and clothing to help non-believers celebrate their holidays. Now even worse things take place.

## Selection 13

وهنا نقف وقفة مع واقعنا . هل نحن فعلا نبيع الوسائل المؤدية ألى الاحتفال بالعيد أو تعظيم أعياد الكفار ؟ أمر مؤلم أن نقول لكم نعم . إن هذا المنكر العظيم منتشر ومتفشٍ في مجتمعنا . وهذه مسألة غير مسألة حضور أعيادهم أو الاحتفال بها . من ذلك مثلا أن المكتبات التجارية ولاسيما في الاسواق المركزية وهذا مشاهد هنا في جدة تبيع البطاقات التي يتهاداها أولئك ويهنّئ بعضُهم بعضا بها . وهذه عشرة نماذج لانواع البطاقات مشتراة من مكتبات متنوعة بالفواتير من مدينة جدة . تركت الاشياء التي هي صور خليعة مثلا أو نساء لكن كلها يجمعها أنها تشتمل على الصلبان . كلها بها الصليب ! لاحظتم !؟ لا يخلو من صليب أو كنيسة فهذا دليل على أنها فعلا من شعائر دينهم ومع ذلك فإنها تباع في مكتبات المسلمين وهذا أمر لا يجوز بأي حال من الاحوال وهو من أعظم المنكرات التي يجب إنكارها

At this point, we [should] stop for a moment [to look at] our reality. Do we actually sell items contributing to holiday celebration or to the glorification of the unbelievers' festivities? It is a painful thing that we [must] say to you: "yes!" This great atrocity is widespread and raging in our society. And, this problem is not [merely] the problem of attending their holidays or celebrating them. A part of this [atrocity] is, for example, that commercial bookstores, especially in central markets -- and this is to be witnessed here in Jiddah, are selling cards which those [unbelievers] exchange as gifts and with which they congratulate each other. These are ten examples of the kinds of cards bought from various bookstores, with receipts, in the city of Jeddah. The kinds which [have] immoral pictures, for example -- or women, have been left out. But all of them have in common that they include crosses. On them all is the cross. Have you noticed!? [Not one of them] is without a cross or [the picture of] a church! Th[ese pictures] are a proof that the[se cards] are, in fact, among the rites of their religion. Despite that [fact], they are sold in Muslims' bookstores. This is an affair which is not permissible in any circumstance, and it is one of the greatest atrocities which must be rejected.

## Selection 14

إن أردتم الدقة في الاحصائيات لتعلموا كم يرد إلى هذه البلاد وكيف
تباع هذه البطاقات وتباع الاشجار التي يسمونها اشجار عيد الميلاد
وما أشبه ذلك فنحن ننقل لكم من نشرة إحصائيات التجارة الخارجية
وهي نشرة رسمية تصدرها مصلحة الاحصاءات العامة بوزارة المالية
كل عام . معروفة ومتداولة وهذا الصنف دائما رقمه ٩٧٠٥ في كل
عام تجدون إذا اخذتم الكتاب انظر رقم ٩٧٠٥ تجدون أنه ما يتعلق
بالاعياد والمهرجانات وأشجار عيد الميلاد بالذات وما يستخدمه الحواة
— الحواة السحرة الذين يتعاملون مع الثعابين بالسحر . لكن أهم شئ
طبعا أهم سلعة هي ما يتعلق بعيد الميلاد وبأشجاره .

If you want to be precise, statistically, so as to know how many come into this country, and how these cards are sold ([and how] the trees which they call "Christmas trees" and other things of that sort are sold), we will convey [some numbers] to you from the *Survey of Foreign Trade Statistics*, it being an official publication which the Office for Public Statistics of the Ministry of Finance issues every year. It is well known and available. This category is always number 9705. Every year you will find ... look [under] number 9705, and you will find that it relates to holidays and festivals and to Christmas trees *per se*, and to what snake charmers use -- snake charmers, magicians who deal with serpents by magic. But the most important thing, of course, is -- the most important commercial article -- is that related to the Christmas holiday and its trees.

## Selection 15

في عام ٨٥ — طبعا احنا توقيتنا الرسمي مع الاسف أكثر إداراتنا تقويمها الرسمي بالتقويم الميلادي أو الجرجوري وهذا نوع من المشابهة كالمشابهة في أعيادهم كالمشاركة فيها كل ما سنذكره إن شاء الله من الادلة يحرمه فهو داخل فيه استعمال أشهرهم وتقويمهم لكن هكذا الواقع على أية حال — في عام ٨٥ ميلادية بلغ ... بلغت قيمة ما استورد ١,٥٨٩,٢٣٣

In the year 1985 .... Of course, our official calendar ... [I'm] sorry [to say] most of our administrative bureaus [use, as] their official calendar, the Christian or Gregorian calendar. And, this kind of imitation is like imitating their holidays, like participating in them. All that we will refer to, God willing, are indications; He forbids them and intervenes in them: using their months and calendar. But, such is reality in any case. During the year of 1985 it reached .... The value of th[ose Christmas trees] which were imported reached 1,589,233 [riyals].

## Selection 16

من المؤلم أيضا والمؤسف يا إخوان أن بعض هذه البطاقات يُطبع في دول خليجية ويستورد منها ولا حول ولا قوة إلا بالله . فأصبحت ... أصبح المسلمون يطبعون هذه الكروت وفيها الصلبان ويبيعونها . وأشد ألماً من ذلك أننا في هذا البلد الطيب — في بلاد التوحيد — نشتري وندخل هذه الأعداد وهذه الارقام . وفي ذلك دليل على أنها رائجة سائرة عندنا من غير إنكار . وأنا لا استبعد أن تكون أيضا بعض المطابع تطبعها هنا في جدة ولاسيما مع قرب الموسم . إذا قرب الموسم — ونظرا لهذه الكميات الهائلة ( ملايين من البطاقات ) والطباعة كما تعلمون لا تكلف ( لاسيما إذا كانت الكمية كبيرة ) — فبدلا أن يستوردها بريالين مثلا أو ما أشبه ذلك يمكن لا تكلفه قرشين إذا طبعها ههنا

Among [those things which are] painful, also, and saddening O brothers is [the fact] that some of these cards are printed in Gulf countries and imported from them. There is no fear and no power save in God! So, they began ... Muslims have begun to print these cards, on them being [pictures of] crosses, and to sell them. [Even] more painful than that is [the fact] that we, in this good country -- in the country of *tawhid*, buy these [huge] numbers and these figures [of such cards]! In these [figures] is an evidence that they are in circulation and common among us without [any] refutation. I do not think it far fetched that some print shops [might] be printing them here in Jiddah especially with the proximity of the season. When the season is approaching -- and in view of these astounding amounts (millions of cards) and printing, as you know, not costing [anything] (especially if the quantity is great) -- rather than import them at two riyals, for instance or something like that, it is possible that they would not cost [the seller] two piasters if he printed them here.

## Selection 17

ولا أحد يخالفك أشد ممن يخالفك في دينك . بل انظروا أضرب لكم مثلا من الواقع انظروا إلى لاعبي الكرة . هل يمكن أن ينزل إلى الميدان فريقان من لاعبي الكرة ويكون لباسهما واحدا وشعارهما واحدا؟ ما يمكن ! لماذا؟ لانهما فريقان متقابلان متصارعان أو متنافسان متباريان . فهل في الدنيا عداوة أشد من عداوة المؤمنين والكافرين — من العداوات التي بينهما؟ وهل من عدوين يجب أن يتباغضا ويتدابرا ويتهاجرا أشد من المؤمنين والكافرين؟ هل هناك نسبة أو تقارب بين أصحاب الصراط المستقيم وأصحاب المغضوب عليهم والضالين ؟ هل هناك تقارب أو تسوية بين من يهدي إلى الجنة وبين من يهدي إلى النار — بين أهل النار وأهل الجنة بين المتقين والفجار؟ لا يمكن أبدا .

No one will differ [with] you more strongly than he who differs [with] you about your religion! Just look. I'll give you an example from reality. Look at soccer players. Is it possible for two teams to go onto the field, their uniforms being the same and their slogans being the same? It is not possible! Why? Because they are two teams confronting each other and struggling or competing and matching [themselves against each other]. Is there, in th[is] world, any enmity greater than the enmity between believers and non-believers -- because of the hostilities which [lie] between them? Are there any two enemies who must hate, oppose, and avoid [each other] more sharply than believers and non-believers? Is there any relationship or closeness between the people of the "Straight Path" and "those against whom God is angry and those gone astray?" Is there any closeness or compatibility between he who guides [others] towards heaven and he who guides [others] towards hell -- between the people of Hell and the people of Heaven, between the God-fearing and the impudent? It is not possible, ever.

## Selection 18

ولا يستطيع أحد الان في أوروبا أو في أمريكا أن يحتفل بعيد من أعياد النازية ولا أن يرتدي شعار النازية ويضعه على صدره ويمشي في الشارع . لماذا ؟ لان النازية في نظرهم عدو لهم . فيا سبحان الله كيف بالعداوة التي هي في الدين وهي التي أمر الله تبارك وتعالى بها . وهي أعظم فرقان يجب أن يكون بين المؤمنين و بين الكافرين .

No one can, now -- in Europe or in America, celebrate any of the Nazi's holidays, wear clothes with Nazi insignia, or wear it[s medals] on his chest and walk the streets. Why? Because the Nazis are, in their view, an enemy of theirs. So, glory be to God, what about the enmity which is [based] upon religion, it being the thing on which God, may He be blessed and exalted, has given His orders!? [That enmity] is the greatest divider which must exist between believers and non-believers.

## Selection 19

فأعياد أهل الكتاب أقر -- أمرنا شرعا أن نقرهم عليها . يعني عندما يدخلون في عقد الذمة نقرهم على دينهم ومن جملة دينهم الاحتفال بأعيادهم . وهذه الشبهة يا إخوان سوف تسمعونها في الجرائد وفي التلفاز وفي الاذاعات وغير ذلك . عندما تأتي هذه الاعياد وتفتح الاذاعات العربية -- إلا ما رحم الله -- تجدها كلها تحتفل بهذه الذكرى . فمن جملة ما يأتي من التفلسف ويبرر يقول إن هذه الاعياد أُقرت -- من جملة دينهم الذي أقر وإن الاسلام يحترم أهل الكتاب وما نحو ذلك . شيخ الاسلام رحمه الله يرد على هذا رداً قويا وأنا أقرأ لكم نصه . قال << المحظور في أعياد أهل الكتابين التي نقرهم عليها أشد من المحظور في أعياد الجاهلية التي لا نقرهم عليها . فإن الامة قد حُذروا من مشابهة اليهود والنصارى . واخبروا أنه سيفعل قوم منهم هذا المحظور بخلاف دين الجاهلية فإنه لا يعود إلا في آخر الدهر عند احترام أنفس المؤمنين عموما.>>

So, the People of the Book's holidays have been acknowledged -- we were ordered, in law, to confirm the[ people of the Book] in the[ir holidays]. I mean, when they enter into a treaty of protection, we confirm them in their religion, and a part of the whole of their religion is the celebration of their holidays. This is a specious argument, O brothers, which you will hear in newspapers, on television, in radio broadcasts and elsewhere. When these holidays come along, and you turn on the Arab radio broadcasts -- unless God has been merciful, you'll find them all celebrating this anniversary. As a part of all the philosophizing which will come along to justify [this, some] will say: "These holidays have been acknowledged; [they are] a part of the whole of their religion which has been acknowledged; Islam respects the people of the Book," and things like that. The Sheikh al-Islam, may God have mercy upon him, has made a strong reply to that. I will read to you the text of [his reply]. He said: "The prohibition [against Muslims participating in] the holidays of the peoples of the two books, to which [holidays] we *do* acknowledge the[ir right], is stronger than the prohibition [against participating in] holidays of the pagan era in which we do *not* confirm the[ polytheists]. The [Muslim] community has been warned about imitating the Jews and the Christians, and the[ Muslims] have been told that a group of the [Jews and Christians] will [continue to] perform this prohibited [act], in contradistinction to the pagan era's religion [which is to be completely suppressed]. But, [acknowledgement] refers only to the end of time when respect for believing souls, generally, [will hold]."

## Selection 20

«طيب هذا النهي يعني ما المقصود فيه ؟ المقصود ما نسميها الان « الفرجة . يعني واحد قال « اليوم عيد النصارى خلينا نروح الكنيسة نتفرج نشوف ايش يساووا » هذا الذي قصده عمر رضي الله تعالى عنه « أما أن يشاركهم المسلم في أعيادهم وأن يهنئهم بها فهذا من دينهم . » لكن هذا الفرجة فلا تدخلوا عليهم لأنها مكان سخط ومكان نزول عذاب -- نسأل الله العفو والعافية -- وغضب من الله . فربما ان يهلكهم الله عز وجل بما يعلنون من الشرك والكفر ويهلك معهم هذا المسلم المؤمن .

Fine, this prohibition ... I mean what is its intention? The intention [has to do with] what we now call "sight-seeing." I mean, [suppose] someone said: "Today is a Christians' holiday. Let's go to church to see ... to have a look at what they are doing." This is what Omar, may God (be He exalted) be pleased with him, meant: "As for the Muslim joining them on their holidays and congratulating them on them, this is of *their* religion." But, this "sight-seeing," don't get in with them because [their church] is a place of wrath, a place [upon which] punishment [may] fall -- we ask forgiveness and health of God, and [a place] for anger from God. God, may He be magnified and glorified, might destroy them for the polytheism and infidelity they proclaim and destroy that Muslim believer [who has gone to sight-see] with them.

Chapter Five

# Internal Divisions

## Introduction

It may be true, as Sheikh Safar al-Hawali says in his lesson "The True Promise and the False One," that "America is [Islam's] worst enemy." It may also be true that the hostility of the U.S. is based on religious doctrine, as he goes on to say. Conflict internal to the Arab-Muslim community in socio- and politico-religious interpretation is also a problem however, and that conflict is of great concern to our Saudi preachers. That concern is expressed, especially, in three lessons in our sample. The issues at stake are explored below through selections from each.

In the tape entitled, "A Dialog with Sheikh Safar al-Hawali," the preacher responds to an unidentified interviewer's questions. Among those questions are a series which focus on the problem of بدعة [bid$^{c}$ah], "heresy." Sheikh Safar's responses are cast in terms of the technicalities of Islamic law. It is clear that the Sheikh yearns to be "liberal" and "inclusive," but many Qur'anic interpretations made by "Modernizers" are, in his view, simply beyond the pale.

In "The Meaning of Bin Baz's Statement," Safar al-Hawali responds to queries he has received about a statement made by Saudi Arabia's Chief Mufti, $^{c}$Abdul-$^{c}$Aziz Bin Baz. Sheikh Safar does not precisely identify which of Bin Baz's several statements on similar matters is in question, and I have not been able to do so through internal evidence. It is clear, however, that Sheikh Safar and his colleagues have sharp critics among Saudi Arabia's $^{c}$*ulama'*, not to mention those whom Sheikh Safar labels "secularists" and "Westernizers." In the tape entitled "The Dregs* of the Kuwaiti Press," it is the journalists of a sister Arab country whom Sheikh Salman al-$^{c}$Awdah confronts.

* Lit. "chaff" هشيم

## Chapter Five

### A Brief Introduction to the Terminology of Islamic Law

Given the legal, technical terminology to be found below, it may be appropriate to give the briefest of introductions to the subject here. Among Muslim religious scholars (sing. عالم [$^{C}$*alim*], pl. علماء [$^{C}$*ulama'*]) in general, the "jurisprudent," (sing. فقيه [*faqih*], pl. فقهاء [*fuqaha'*]) in particular, *derives* "God's law" (شريعة [*shari*$^{C}$*ah*]) from the Qur'an and the Sunnah of the Prophet. The latter is to be found in the "cannonical collections" of "traditions" (sing. حديث [*hadith*], pl. أحاديث [*'ahadith*]) which are "narrative reports of the sayings, deeds, and 'silent affirmations' of the Prophet." Interpretations of the Qur'an and the Sunnah are validated by "consensus" (إجماع [*'ijma*$^{C}$]) in the scholarly community; a *hadith* says, "My Community will never agree upon error." "Analogical reasoning" (قياس [*qiyas*]) is used to extrapolate from the Qur'an and Sunnah when no specific provision is to be found in them. The Qur'an, Sunnah, consensus, and analogical reasoning are the "principles of jurisprudence" (أصول الفقه [*'usuwl al-fiqh*]; *'usuwl* is literally "roots" and often translated as "sources."

The process of interpreting the Qur'an and Sunnah, drawing analogies from them, and gathering consensus for an interpretation or analogy is "jurisprudential endeavor" (اجتهاد [*'ijtihad*]). It is what the *faqih* does; he is, therefore, a *mujtahid* (مجتهد) though this term is most closely associated with Shi$^{C}$i Islam. The products of the *'ijtihad* of the *fuqaha'* may be found in *fiqh* manuals, but they are most prominently published as "legal opinions" (sing. فتوى [*fatwa*], pl. فتاوى [fatawa]) in response to questions on specific points of law from judges (sing. قاض [*qadi*], pl قضاة [*qudat*]), lawyers (sing. محام [*muhami*] pl. محامون [*muhamuwn*]), parties to cases, or other interested individuals. The *fatwas* of particularly influential *fuqaha'* are gathered up and published in popular collections. The law contained in *fiqh* manuals and *fatwa* collections are known as the law's "branches" (فروع [furu$^{C}$]) as opposed to the "roots of the law" mentioned above.

## Part 1

## "Dispute or Heresy?" from *A Dialogue with Sheikh Safar al-Hawali* by Safar al-Hawali

### Selection 1

شيخ سفر هناك من يُثير دعوى << لا إنكار في مسائل الخلاف >> . فهل هذه القاعدة صحيحة وعلى إطلاقها؟ ولماذ يتكئ عليها دعاة عصرنا اليوم؟

[Interviewer:] Sheikh Safar there are those who stir up the claim [that]: "there is no sin in questions of *khilaf*."* Is that principle correct, absolutely? And why is [the principle] being used† in our era, today?

* The term خلاف [*khilaf*], "difference, dispute" is used here in its technical, legal sense meaning: "a legitimate difference of opinion among religious scholars;" "a point of legal dispute." According to a well known *hadith*, the Prophet says: "Legitimate differences in religious-legal interpretation are a blessing from God." That is, the tension between خلاف "dispute" and إجماع "consensus," is a creative one leading to equity and justice.

† Lit. "depended upon;" VIII وكأ .

### Selection 2

الحمد لله والصلاة والسلام على رسول الله وبعد . فإن القول بأنه << لا أنكار في مسائل الخلاف >> هذا قول قديم مأثور تداوله بعض العلماء من قبل . ولكنه يُستخدم الآن لأغراض خبيثة أوسع وأبعد مما كان من قبل — كغيره من المصطلحات ومن القواعد التي تُوسّع فيها في هذا الزمن لغرض إفساد هذا الدين .

[Sheikh Safar:] Praise be to God, and blessings and peace be upon His Messenger. Now thereafter: The statement that "there is no sin in issues of *khilaf* " is an old one handed down [from earlier generations] about which several scholars have gone round and round before. But, it is being used now for vile, broader and further-reaching purposes than it was before -- like other terms and principles [the meanings of] which are being expanded upon at this time for the purpose of corrupting [our] religion.

## Selection 3

ولا شك أن هذا المصطلح — أو هذه القاعدة — ليست على إطلاقها . فإن الخلاف ... ليس كل خلاف يعتبر ... فإن ... وليس كل خلاف يعتذر كما ذكر ذلك العلماء ... الثقات من علماء ... أهل السنة والجماعة . فالخلاف قد يكون غير جائز — كمن يخالف نصاً من كتاب الله أو سنة رسول الله ( صلى الله عليه وسلم ) أو إجماع السلف الصالح .

There is no doubt that this term -- or this principle -- is not absolute. Not every *khilaf* is considered [legitimate] ... even if .... not every *khilaf* is to be excused, as scholars ... trustworthy scholars among the people of the *Sunnah* and *Jama*$^{c}$*ah* have said. The "dispute[d point]" might not be permissible, as [is the case with] he who disagrees with a text from the *Book of God* , the *Sunnah* of the Prophet (may God bless him and grant him peace), or the consensus of [our] worthy ancestors.

## Selection 4

وهذا لا يعني أن المخالف نفسه لا يكون مأجوراً . فقد يكون مخالف مأجوراً وقد بذل وسعه وطاقته وجهده في الوصول للحق . ولكن هذا هو غاية ما وصل اليه بحثه ونظره واجتهاده .

This does not mean that the disputant, himself, is not rewarded [by God in heaven]. There may be a rewarded disputant, he having exerted [all] his capacity, power and effort towards arriving at the truth, but this [incorrect interpretation] is the most that his research, his vision and his *'ijtihad* has reached.*

* There is a well-known *hadith* to the effect that "Those who interpret the Qur'an correctly receive two rewards in heaven while those who interpret in good faith, even if incorrectly, still get one."

## Selection 5

لكن لا يجوز لمن علم أنه لا دليل له إلا هذا أن يخالف الدليل الصحيح الثابت أو إذا كان الخلاف في الدلالة لا يجوز له أن يخالف الدليل القطعي الدلالة لوجود خلاف سابق ويقول إن المسألة خلافية . فالرجوع هو -- كما أمر الله تبارك وتعالى عند الخلاف -- إنما يكون إلى كتاب الله وإلى سنة رسول الله صلى الله عليه وسلم .

But, it is not permissible, for someone who has come to know that he has no evidence but this [weak sort of argument], to dispute true, firm evidence. Or, if the dispute is about meaning, it is not permissible to dispute decisively defined* evidence because of the existence of an earlier dispute and to say: "The problem is "disputational."[†] Reference[‡] *is* -- as God (may He be blessed and exalted) has ordered, in case of dispute -- rather [reference] *shall be* to *God's Book* and the *Tradition* of God's messenger, may God bless him and grant him peace.

* Note the "adjectival" or "false" construct [ إضافة غير حقيقية ] here-- الدليل القطعي الدلالة . Lit. "the decisive-of-meaning evidence."

† Note the use of the نسبة adjective here. Lit. "the problem is *related to* the technical, legal matter of *khilaf*."

‡ I.e. one must "return to" God's Book and the Sunnah for the resolution of disputes on their meaning.

## Selection 6

وأما هؤلاء العصريون أو العصرانيون وأمثالهم فهؤلاء ينطبق عليهم أكثر ما ينطبق المقولة السابقة وهي أنه من تتبع رُخص العلماء تزندق. فهؤلاء يأتون إلى كل مسألة من مسائل العلم يقولون << هذه خلافية .>> و <<هذه فيها خلاف .>> وتتشعب هذه الامور حتى لا تنتهي الامة إلى شئ .

As for these contemporaries or "modernists" and their likes, even more of the preceding statement is to be applied to them, that being: "those who follow slack scholars, fall into atheism." These [modernists] come to every question of law* saying: "This is disputational,"† and "there is legitimate disagreement on that." These issues become so muddled that the community [can]not come to a conclusion on anything.

* Lit. "knowledge"; contemporaneously "science."

† I.e. "open to legitimate difference."

## Selection 7

فيقول ارجعوا إلى الشريعة الاسلامية دون التقيد بمذهب معين بل بما يتفق مع روح هذا القانون بما يتفق مع روح هذا القانون دون التقيد بمذهب معين ولو كان زيديا ولو كان رافضياً ولو كان ظاهرياً ولو كان قولاً ضعيفاً أُثر من قبل . وهذه تفتح باباً عظيماً من أبواب الضلال على الامة وتشتت وحدتها العملية كما أنها تشتت وحدتها الفكرية والنظرية .

[Some one of these modernists might] say: "go back to [the sources of] Islamic law without being bound to a[ny] specific school [of law].* Rather, [go back to] that which agrees with the spirit of this law -- that which agrees with the spirit of this law without being bound to any specific school, even if it be Zaidi, or if it be Rafidi, or if it be Zahiri,† even if it be [based on] a weak statement already tracked down [and shown to be weak]‡ This opens a huge door to being led astray before the community. [Such a practice] breaks up [the community's] operative unity just as it breaks up its unity of thought and theory.

* This reference suggests the practice of تلفيق [talfiq] --"patching together" or "drumming up" -- commonly used in contemporary *shari^c^ah* courts. Legal precepts are drawn from the doctrines any of the four different "schools of law," without reference to doctrinal consistency. They are intermixed with those of the other schools and applied to the case at hand as required by the Judge's sense of equity. The reference also calls to mind, however, another, larger and extremely complex issue. For many Muslims, the idea of "going back to the sources" suggests dispensing with the ^C^*ulama'* and doing one's own interpretation. Wherein then lies "consensus"? Is it the consensus of the scholars or of the community at large? Even the most radical of the ^C^*ulama'* take a rather conservative view on this matter as we may see in Sheikh Safar's comments.

† The terms Zaidi, Rafidi and Zahiri refer to "schools of law" which Sheikh finds deplorable. Only

the Zaidi currently exists (in Yemen). The Zaidi and Rafidi schools are Shi[c]ite, explaining Sheikh Safar's disdain. The Zahiri school was founded by Ibn Hazm in Spain in the 10th century AD. It is long defunct. It was highly literalist, and one might expect Sheikh Safar to find antecedents of his own positions in it (as others have indeed done). The Zahiris did, however, also come to some remarkably "progressive" conclusions which might explain Sheikh Safar's lumping the Zahiris together with the Zaidis and Rafidis to indicate that the "modernists" don't even adhere to the most wild schools of interpretation. Elsewhere below, Sheikh uses "Rafidi" as a perjorative term for contemporary Shi[c]i Muslims.

‡ Hadiths were examined in the early centuries of Islam. Those found to be authentic were gathered into canonical collections upon which legal scholars might depend. Not all were given the same weight however. A continuum of validity was established. It runs from the most strongly attested statements which are termed "sound" [ صحيح ] to those most poorly attested labeled "weak" [ضعيف].

## Selection 8

ولكن يا شيخ مفهوم هذا أن الخلاف لابد أن يبقى في الامة . فهل يمكن أن نقول إن هناك مواضيع يجوز أن يحدث فيها الخلاف ومواضيع لا يجوز أن يحدث فيها الخلاف ؟

[Interviewer:] But Sheikh, the significance of this is that dispute must [always] persist in the community. Can we say that there are subjects on which disagreement is permissible and subjects on which dispute is impermissible?

## Selection 9

نعم الخلاف باقٍ . << ولا يزالون مختلفين >> كما ذكر الله تبارك وتعالى سواء كانَ في العقائد أو في الفروع . وكلامنا نحن الآن هو في الفروع ... في الاستدلال طبعاً الخلاف باقٍ . ولكن يسوغ أو يصح ويجوز في مواضع الاجتهاد وموارد الاجتهاد وهي كثيرة جداً . فيما يسميه العلماء ... علماء الأصول ... تحقيق المناط هذا وارد لأن نتفق جميعاً على النص الشرعي من الكتاب أو السنة أو الاجماع أيضا أو القياس الصحيح أيضا . قد نتفق على هذه ولكن نختلف في تحقيق مناط هذا الدليل الصحيح سواء كان كتاباً أو سنة أو قياساً او إجماعاً . فهذا — نعم — هذا سائغ ووارد . لابد أن تختلف فيه الأنظار . هذا طبيعي وهذا من حكمة الله تبارك وتعالى .

[Sheikh Safar:] Yes, difference[s] persist. "They will not cease disputing,"* as He, may He be blessed and exalted, said, whether it be on [points of] doctrine or on secondary issues.† What we are talking about now are secondary issues ... in seeking out meaning, of course, dispute will persist, but it is to be shaped or corrected and it is permissible on points [admissible of] Ijtihad and sources for Ijtihad, and they are very numerous. As for what scholars -- scholars of "the sources [of jurisprudence"] -- call "object verification," it occurs because we all agree on legal provision[s] from the Book, Sunnah, consensus also or sound analogy also. We may agree on these but disagree on the object verification of [a specific piece of] sound evidence, whether it be from the Book, Sunnah, analogy or consensus. So this -- yes -- this is allowable, and it does come up. Viewpoints must differ on [such things]. This is natural; this is part of the wisdom of God, may He be blessed and exalted.

* Qur'an 11:118.
† Lit. "branches" and set off against أصول ['usuwl] "roots" as used below.

## Selection 10

فإن دخل منهج بعض هذه الجماعات أو التجمعات شئ من الخلل فهل يخرجون من اسم أو مسمى أهل السنة والجماعة ؟

[Interviewer:] If there entered ... if any type of defect were to enter the program of any one of these groups or associations, would they be expelled from the appellation or designation "People of the Sunnah and Jama^c^ah?"

## Selection 11

نعم . العدل في هذا الامر هو كما نرى ونعلم من مناهج — نعم — وطريقة السلف الصالح ( رضوان الله تعالى عليهم ) في الجرح والتعديل . وهو أن الاعتبار إنما يكون بالمسلك والمنهج وأصله بالطريقة والتمسك والاتباع . فمن كان متبعاً لكتاب الله وسنة رسوله ( صلى الله عليه وسلم ) وللسلف الصالح في الجملة والاصل متحرياً للحق مجتهداً في إقتفاء آثارهم فإنه يكون منهم أي من أهل السنة والجماعة ومن إتباع السلف الصالح وإن أخطأ . فإنه ليس بمجرد انتساب الانسان إلى أهل السنة أو إلى السلف يكون معصوماً . بل ما يزال كل بشر عرضة للخطأ فمهما أخطأ في بعض الامور فإنه

يظل من اهل السنة والجماعة . أما إذا كان الخلاف عن أتباع لاصل من أصول أهل البدع فإنه يلحقه ما يلحق أهل ذلك الاصل من الذم أو اللوم أو القدح أو الطعن . منها ما قد يكون مخرجاً من الملة — يسأل الله العفو والعافية . ومنها ما يكون صاحبه مبتدعاً ضالاً مذموماً بحسب درجته .

[Sheikh Safar:] Yes. Justice, in this issue, is (as we see and know) in programmatics -- yes -- and [in] [our] worthy Ancestors' way (may God's pleasure -- be He exalted -- be with them) [as expressed] in the "Wounding and Justification" [literature].* [Justice] is that considering [one to be a member of a group] may only be through [that person's adherence to the group's] method, program -- promoting [it's] path, holding tight [to its beliefs], and following [its doctrine]. Whoever is a follower of God's Book, the Prophet's Sunnah (may God bless him and grant him peace), and of [our] Righteous Ancestors, in everything and in principle -- seeking out the Truth, striving to follow their footsteps -- such person will be one of them, that is [one] of the People of the Sunnah and Jama$^{c}$ah and one of the followers of [our] Righteous Ancestors even if he makes a mistake. But, a person, by his mere affiliation with the People of the Sunnah and Jama$^{c}$ah or with [our] ancestors is not infallible. Rather, every human is still open to error. But, however much he may make mistakes in some matters, he remains [a member] of the People of the Sunnah and Jama$^{c}$ah. Should, however, the conflict be about following one of the principles of the People of Heresy, then that censure, blame, rebuke, or vilification which befalls the people of that principle will befall him. Among [the things which might befall him] are that he may be expelled from [our] sect -- may he ask God for forgiveness and protection. And, among [those things that might befall him] is that his companion may be [only] a heretical innovator, one gone astray, one rebuked in accord with his degree [of sinfulness].†

* That branch of biographical literature which examines the character of persons involved in transmitting *hadiths*.

† I.e. he no longer has any relationship with believers, only with nonbelievers.

### Selection 12

وعلى هذا الاساس يكون أيضاً التعامل . إذا قررنا هذا الاصل واعتبرناهم مسلمين فإن لهم حق — الحق الذي للمسلم على المسلم . ولكن أيضاً يبغضون ويرد عليهم وتُكره بدعهم وضلالتهم وتحارب وتنصح الامة منهم . فلا يُهدر حقهم بالكلية فيكونون كالكفار ولا يعطون الولاء الكامل كمن هو على الكتاب والسنة.

On this basis, too, is to be mutual interaction [among people]. If we decide [in favor of] this principle, and we consider them to be Muslims, they have a certain right -- the right [due] to one Muslim from [another] Muslim. But, they are also to be hated and restrained; their heresy and their misguidance are to be despised and fought against, and the community is to be warned against them. Their due is not to be withdrawn totally such that they be like infidels, but they are not to be given complete friendship like he who is [in harmony] with the Book and the Sunnah.

### Selection 13

أما على الاعتبار الاخر إذا قلنا أنهم يعنى أهل البدع أو أهل الضلال هؤلاء خارجون عن الملة فهؤلاء يأخذون حكم الكفار . البدع المغلطة كبدع الخوارج مثلاً وما أشبهها ... هؤلاء جاء فيهم النص عن رسول الله صلى عليه وسلم بقتالهم . وهذه قاعدة أصل عظيم مندرج فيه قاعدة قتال أهل البدع أو من التعامل مع أهل البدع أيضاً — قتالهم وهجرهم ونبذهم وهذا كله وارد .

As for the other possibility,* if we say they are, I mean, the people of heresy or people gone astray, [then] they are outside of the sect; then they take on the legal status of infidels. Serious heresies (like the Kharijites'† heresies -- for example -- and those similar to them) ... those [people], a text by the Prophet of God (may God bless him and grant him peace) about fighting them has come out about them.‡ This a principle, a great source included in it being a principle [on] fighting against the people of heresy or about dealing with the people of heresy too -- fighting them, expelling them, ostracizing them -- all of this comes up [in the Qur'an and Sunnah].

* Lit. "consideration" as set off against the possibility discussed in the preceding paragraph.

† Early Islamic schismatics particularly hostile to [c]Ali's cause and a contemporary byword of extreme opprobrium for one's Muslim opponents.

‡ This is a rather complex "topic-comment" sentence.

## Selection 14

لكن ذلك لا يُضيّع ما لهم من حق الاسلام ما داموا مسلمين . كما قال عليّ رضي الله تعالى عنه لهم لما قالوا << لا حكم إلا لله >> — صاحوا في جنبات المسجد — قال << إن لكم علينا ثلاثة — ألا نمنعكم مساجد الله وألا نمنعكم من فئ الله وألا نبدأكم بقتال . >> هذا حق للمسلم ما دام مسلم مع كشف شبهته وبيان ضلاله وخطأه وردعه وهجره بالاسلوب الشرعي .

But that does not dissipate that right [in] Islam which they have as long as they [remain] Muslims. As [c]Ali (may God -- be He exalted-- be pleased with him) said to the[ Kharijites], when they said "No judgement save in God" -- they yelled in the corners of the Mosque-- he said: "You are owed three [things] by us: that we not forbid you God's Mosques; that we not deny you God's share*, and that we not start a fight against you." This is a Muslim's right as long as he is a Muslim, along with disclosing his sophism, displaying his having gone astray and his error, and curbing him and avoiding him in the lawful way.

* That share of booty gained in "fighting in God's way" and distributed among all soldiers involved in the battle.

# Chapter Five

## Part 2

**"Sheikh vs. Sheikh"** from ***The Meaning of Bin Baz's Statement*** by **Safar al-Hawali.**

### Selection 1

يطلب كثير من الاخوة -- كما ترون بهذه الرسائل -- إيضاح حقيقته أو المراد به أو-- كما يعبرون-- وضع النقاط على الحروف فيه وهو البيان الذي أصدره سماحة الوالد الشيخ عبد العزيز بن عبد الله ابن باز حفظه الله وجزاه الله عن الاسلام والمسلمين وعن الدعاة وعن طلبة العلم خير الجزاء . فهو اب كريم وموجّه ومربٍ حكيم . وهو ناصح مُشفق وهو الذي رتّب هذه البرامج الدعوية . وتخرّجت هذه الأجيال على يَديه وبأثر علمه . وهو الذي ذب عن أعراضهم لما رأى النيل و القدح والطعن فيها . فهو جدير أن يشكر بعد شكر الله تبارك و تعالى.

Many brothers have requested -- as you can see from these letters -- a clarification of [the] truth [of the statement], or what was meant by it, or -- as they express [it] -- "dotting its i's [and crossing its t's],"* "it" being the statement which his eminence, [our] father Sheikh $^{C}$Abd al-$^{C}$Aziz Bin $^{C}$Abd-Allah Bin Baz (may God preserve him and requite him [with] the best of rewards) has issued on Islam, the Muslims, preachers, and seekers of knowledge. He is a generous father, a guide, and a wise instructor. He is a kind adviser, and he is the one who has organized these preaching programs. These generations† have graduated under his tutelage‡ and under the influence of his knowledge. He is the one who has defended their dignity when he saw it being offended, defamed, and damaged. So, he deserves to be thanked -- after thanking God (may He be blessed and exalted).

* Lit. "putting the dots on its letters."

† Self referential. I.e. the recent graduates of the religious universities, including the speaker.

‡ Lit. "at his hands."

## Selection 2

لكن الموجب لهذا الإيضاح ... الموجب هو سوء الفهم والتفسير والتدليس الذي حصل نتيجة هذا البيان الذي أراد به سماحته أن يكون كالماء يطفئ النار. وهوكذلك والحمد لله. فإن كل طلاب العلم والحمد لله — وأنتم منهم و تعلمون ذلك — قد عرفوا ماذا يريد الشيخ ومن يقصد وأطفأ الفتنة والحمد لله وأظهر الحق وأبانه ودافع عن المظلومين والمهضومين ونصح المعتدين والباغين بأجدى وأوضح بيان وعبارة .

But, the imperative for this clarification ... the imperative is the misunderstanding, [poor] interpretation and falsification that happened as a result of this statement which his eminence intended to be like water extinguishing fire. And, it has been like that, praise be to God. All students (praise be to God) -- and you are among them, and you know that -- have understood what the Sheikh wants and whom he means. He has put out the sedition, praise be to God. He has demonstrated the truth and displayed it; [he has] defended the unjustly accused and the oppressed; he has advised the aggressors and offenders through the most useful and clear statement and expression.

## Selection 3

لكن لوجود بعض محامل السوء والتدليس سواء ما ظهر في بعض عناوين من عناوين في بعض الجرائد — نقولها مع الاسف — أو كذلك من بعض الناس الذين افتروا افتراءات عجيبة وإن كانت نادرة وقليلة ولا يقبلها عاقل يعني كقولهم إن الشيخ أراد بهذا الرد على الدعاة والانتصار للعلمانين والعياذ بالله هل يعقل هذا ؟

But, because of the presence of some of those who bear evil and falsehood, as well as what has appeared in some headlines in some newspapers -- we say it sadly -- or likewise from some people who have fabricated strange concoctions, even though it was rare and slight and no rational [person] would accept it.... I mean, like their statement that the Sheikh wanted, in this [statement], to refute the preachers and defend the secularists! All refuge is in God! Is it rational?*

* All of this in introductory to the next statement.

## Selection 4

فلذلك نقول إن المقصود أيها الإخوة بهذا هم فئة معدودة محدودة قليلة
جداً — والحمد لله — من الدعاة كما بينه حفظه الله . لأنه قال << إن
كثيراً من المنتسبين إلى العلم والدعوة . >> إذاً قضية دعاة وطلاب
علم. هذه فئه قليله جداً يقعون في أعراض كثير من إخوانهم الدعاة
المشهورين .

For that reason, we say: "[his] meaning, O brothers, in this [statement] is a [certain] group, a limited, restricted, very small -- praise be to God -- [group] of preachers, as he made clear (may God preserve him)." Because, he said: "*many* of those associated with learning and the *da$^{c}$wah* ." Therefore, it is a matter of preachers and students. This is a very small group defaming the honor of many of their brothers, the famous preachers.

## Selection 5

فالقضية بين الدعاة . لا دخل لا للعلمانين ولا للخرافيين ولا للمشركين
. ودعاة الشرك ليسوا من الدعاة ولا من إخوان الدعاة و إنما هم أعداء
الدعوة . هذا واضح . إذاً ما الذي فعل هؤلاء ؟ وقعوا في أعراض
إخوانهم طلبة العلم الدعاة المشهورين . ولا بأس أن نسمي لأنه إن لم
نسم فلا تتضح الحقيقة . الدعاة المشهورين الذين تكلم في حقهم هم
فضيلة الشيخ الأخ سلمان العودة حفظه الله وفضيلة الأخ الشيخ عائد
القرني حفظه الله وفضيلة الاخ الشيخ ناصر العمر حفظه الله وفي
العبد الفقير الذي أمامكم الآن . وكذلك تكلم في أعراض كثير من الدعاة
حتى لم يكد يسلم أحد من هؤلاء الناس والادلة موجودة

The matter is between preachers. Secularists, superstitious people, and polytheists have no involvement [in it]. The preachers of polytheism are neither preachers, nor the brothers of preachers. Rather they are the enemies of the *da$^{c}$wah.* This is clear. What is it then that these [people] did? They defamed the honor of their brothers, the seekers of knowledge, the famous preachers. There is no harm [in] naming [them] because if we do not name [them], the truth will not be clear. The famous preachers in whose defense [Bin Baz] spoke are: his grace brother Sheikh Salman al-$^{C}$Awdah (may God preserve him); his grace brother Sheikh

[C]A'ed al-Qarni (may God preserve him), his grace brother Sheikh Naser al-[C]Umar (may God preserve him), and the humble servant who [stands] before you now. Likewise, he spoke about the honor of many preachers even to the extent that scarcely any one of those people was spared, and the evidence is there.

## Selection 6

و يَحْرصون دائماً على الصغار أو المبتدئين أو حديثي العهد بالدعوة ويجلسون ويقولون لهم « فلان وفلان وفلان » ويأتون بألوان من التهم والظلم والبهتان والافتراء الذي يعلم الله سبحانه وتعالى — ويعلم خلقه الذين من أمثالكم يسمعون ويحضرون هذه المحاضرات — أن هذا كذب وزور وافتراء واختلاق ليس له أي أساس من الصحة . هذا يفعلونه سراً في مجالسهم وربما سجلوه في أشرطة تُنشر على الناس وجدوا أن هذا لا يكفي فأصبحوا يسجلون ما في الجلسة ثمّ ينشرونه على الناس . يأتي شاب قد يكون حديث عهد بالاهتداء يريد أن يعرف الحق ويريد أن يعرف طريق الجنة وطريق النار . يقال له خذ هذا الشريط . خذ واسمع . يذهب يسمع . ماذا ينتج؟ ماذا يحصل لديه إذا سمع الطعن في فلان وفلان وفلان ؟ أيهتدي ؟ أنشدكم بالله وكل مؤمن أن تفكروا في هذا ! هل يهتدي ؟ هل يحب الدعاة ؟ هل يخلص لله ؟ هل يقنت في طاعة الله ؟ هل يحس بالخشوع في صلاته ؟ هل يقبل على قراءة القرآن برغبة عندما يسمع هذه الطعون في العلماء والدعاة والمشايخ الذين كل الناس من حوله يتحدثون عنهم ويسمعون لهم ويتأثرون بهم ويزدادون إيمانا إذا سمعوا كلامهم ؟ كيف تبلبل ذهنه ؟ كيف يكون؟

They always take an interest in youngsters or beginners or those who are recently committed to preaching. They sit down and say to them: "such and so and such and so and such and so." They come up with [all] kinds of accusations, injustice, falsehood and lying which God, may He be glorified and exalted, knows -- and his creatures who are the likes of you listening [to tapes] and attending these lectures know -- that this is lying, false, fabrication, and made up; it has no basis in fact. They do this secretly, in their meetings, and perhaps they record it on tapes which are distributed to the people. They've found that this is not enough, so they began to record what [is taking place] in the session[s like this] and distribute [those tapes] to the people. A young man comes along who may be new[ly] committed to seeking divine guidance, wanting to know the Truth, wanting to know the road to Heaven from road to Hell. He's told: "Take this tape. Take [it] and listen." He goes, and he listens. What results? What happens when he's heard the defamation of so-and-so or so-and-so or so-and-so? Is he rightly guided? I appeal to you, by God, and [to] every believer to think about this! Is he rightly guided? Will he love preachers? Will he be loyal? Will he be submissive in obedience to God? Will he feel humility during his prayer? Will he take interest in reading the Koran out of desire when he hears this slander of scholars, preachers, and sheikhs, whom all the people around him are talking about, listening to, and being influenced by, and becoming increasingly faithful whenever they listen to their speech? How [seriously] will his mind be confused? How [troubled should his mind] be?

## Selection 7

هذا الكلام — بما فيه من بهتان وظلم — يمرض قلوب الخاصة . وقد شكى والله بعض العلماء الكبار . قال « لما سمعت هذا والله تأثرت وتألمت وتنكدت » و هو من العلماء الذين يعرفون الحمد لله درجة عالية من العلم . فكيف بطالب علم مبتدئ ؟ ماذا تتوقعون أن يكون أثر مثل هذا الكلام على هذا المسكين في عبادته ؟ في إيمانه؟ قد ينتكس . وحصل وكتب الىّ أن بعض حالات الانتكاس حصلت . هل كنا نثق في هؤلاء؟ إذاً لا خير في أولئك جميعا . وخاصة أن طاعنين مجهولون . يعني أول مرة تجلس معهم أو ربما يعنيٍ مرات فهذا يطعن في المعروف الموثوق والنتيجة أنك تختار هذا قطعاً . بل انت عادة اذا سمعت إنسانا يشكوا ويخاصم إنسانا تبدأ ... ايش ؟ تتحفظ فيما يقول عنه بأنك تعلم أن هذا من منطلق عداوة وخصومة .

This [kind of] talk -- with that falsehood and injustice in it -- will sicken the hearts of the elite. A certain one of the senior scholars, by God, has complained. He said: "When I heard th[at], by God, I was shocked; I was pained; I was made miserable." He is one of the scholars who has, praise be to God, attained a high degree of learning. How [do you think it would effect] a new student? What would you expect the effect of this talk to be on this poor [person's] worship? On his faith? He might backslide. It has happened; it has been written to me that, [in] some circumstances, backsliding has occurred. Would we trust those [people]? Therefore, there is no good in any of those [people]. Especially [in] that the slanderers are unknown. I mean, the first time you sit down with them, or maybe few a times, and then [some person] defames a well known and trusted [person]. The result is that you choose this one, this is certain. Indeed, you usually (if you hear a person complaining [about] and being hostile towards [another] person) start to ... what? You start to be cautious of what [the former] says about [the latter] because you know that this [kind of talk] is from a position of enmity and hostility.

## Selection 8

هذا الذي عبر عنه أحد العلماء لما سمع احد الناس يقع في أعراض العلماء. قال له << يا بني قاتلت الروم ؟ >> قال << لا >> قال << قاتلت الترك أو الديلم ؟>> قال << لا >> قال << سلم منك الروم والترك والديلم ولم يسلم منك المسلمون ؟ سبحان الله ! >> هؤلاء الناس هل قاتلوا أو هل ردوا ووزعوا الأشرطة على أهل البدع ؟

This is what one of the scholars said when he heard a person slandering the honor of scholars. He said: "My son have you fought the Byzantines? He said: 'No.' He said: 'Have you fought the Turks or the Dailamites'? He said: 'No.' He said: 'The Byzantines, Turks and Dailamites have been left alone by you, but the Muslims are not'?! Glory to God!" These people, have they fought or refuted or distributed tapes to the people of heresy?!

## Selection 9

الرافضة يشكلون الربع إلى ثلث من أهل المدينة كما تعلمون . هل ردوا عليهم ودسوا هذه الاشرطة واجتهدوا فيها مثلا سراً أو جهراً وأوصلوها إلى بيوتهم ليبينوا ما هم عليه من الشرك والضلال ما فعلوا ذلك

The Rafidites* make up a quarter to third of the people of Medina, as you know. Have they refuted them and delivered these tapes [to them]? [Have] they exerted themselves with th[e tapes] privately or publicly and brought the[ tapes] to the [Rafidites] houses to explain what kind of polytheism and error they are [involved] in? They have not done that.

* Here the reference is clearly to the Shiʿites of Saudi Arabia.

## Selection 10

هل ردوا على الصوفية وأشباههم ؟ هل ردوا على أعداء السنة
الحقيقين ؟ سمعتم ماذا قالوا ؟ الذي يقول << لحيتي مثل سيف .>>
الذي يقول <<كل ما عندهم حدثنا كحكوح بن سمعان >> إلى آخر ما
سمعتم في صحف تنشر مليون نسخة ومليون ونصف نسخة فيكون
فيها استهزاء بالسنة والاخر يدافع عن ابي رية ويقول << مجتهد >> —
الذي أبطل سنة النبي صلى الله عليه وسلم

Have they refuted the Sufis and their likes? Have they refuted the real enemies of the Sunnah? Have you heard what they've said? The one who says: "My beard is like a sword!?" The one who says: "Everything that they have, Kahkuwh Ibn Sama$^{C}$an has related to us!?" And so on that you've heard in newspapers publishing a million or a million and a half copies in some of which is [to be found] ridicule of the Sunnah while the other [part of the total] defends Abu Ray and calls [him] a *mujtahid* -- the one who denied the Sunnah of the Prophet (may God bless him and grant him peace).

## Selection 11

أما الاعتداء والهجوم والظلم والعدوان بغير سبب وبغير مبرر فهذا
فعلا هو من مقاتلة أهل الاسلام وترك أهل الأوثان . نسأل الله العفو
والعافية . ثم أيضا من صفات الخوارج . نحن لا نقول أنهم خوارج كما
قالوا في حقنا لكن نبين من أقرب الناس

As for hostility, attack, injustice, and enmity -- without reason and without justification -- that is indeed war [against] the people of Islam, and leaving the people of idols alone. We ask God's forgiveness and protection. Then too, [these are some] of the characteristics of the Khawarij. We don't say that they are Khawarij, as they've said about us, but we're [just] explaining who is closerst to the people.

## Selection 12

وقد يفعلونه علانية كما قال الشيخ في محاضرات عامة في المساجد وقد فعلوا ذلك علانية ومنها شريط معلن موجه إليّ بعنوان << نصيحة إلى فلان >> وربما سمعتموه . ومنها أيضا الرد على الشيخ سلمان في شريطه << جلسة على الرصيف >> وغيرها هذه أيضا مما عملوه وفعلوه علانية والله تعالى حسبهم في ذلك

They may do it publicly, as the Sheikh said, in public lectures in mosques. And, they have done that publicly. Among [such actions] is an open tape addressed to me with the title "Advice to So-and-So." Perhaps you've heard it. Also among [such things] is a refutation of Sheikh Salman in his tape "A Session on the Sidewalk" and others. These are among [the things] which they have done publicly. May God, may he be exalted, hold them accountable for that.

## Selection 13

تصوروا عندما تستمع إلى شريط -- دبلجوا أشرطة -- شيخ يتكلم وشيخ آخر يرد عليه . وهذا يقول الكلمة وهذا يرد عليه . أليس هذا هو المقصود ؟ يعني فعلا كم يحصل من الشتات ومن الفرقة ومن القيل والقال . ومن يسمع الشريط فإنه لا يخلو أما أن يؤيد هذا أو يؤيد ذاك مع أن كلا ... كليهما يعني كل منهما ليس مخالفاً للاخر . مثلا محاضرة القيت قبل أربع أو خمس سنوات اقتطع منهاعبارة ومحاضر آخر في موضوع آخر ألقي في مكان آخر بعد سنوات اقتطع منها عبارة . ضربت هذه بهذه . ما النتيجة ؟ لو جلس المحاضران ما اختلفاولتناسقا ولتكلما . لكن لما ضربت العبارة أحدثت بلبلة فيأتي شاب مبتدئ طالب علم يسمع هذا يستغرب ويندهش وينتكس كما قلنا قد ينتكس

Imagine when you listen to a tape -- they've reduplicated tapes --one Sheikh talking and another Sheikh refuting him. The former says [a] word and the latter refutes it. Isn't this the aim? I mean, how many a dispute, division, a back and forth occurs!? And, he who listens to the tape will not be able to avoid either supporting the former or the latter, even though both ... both of them, I mean, each one of them is not in conflict with the other. For example, [there was] a lecture which was delivered four or five years ago; a phrase was cut out of it, and another lecturer -- on another issue which was given in some other place years later -- a phrase was cut out of it. The first was stuck to the latter. What's the result? If the two lecturers sat down together, they would not differ, or they would come to accord or talk. But, when the phrase[s were] stuck together, it created confusion. So, a young man, a beginner -- a student, comes along; he hears this; he's astounded; he's amazed, and he slips back. As we said, he might backslide.

## Selection 14

قالوا إن هؤلاء ليسوا على عقيدة أهل السنة والجماعة إنما يتخذون العقيدة وسيلة ومطية لما يريدون أعوذ بالله الكفار الكفار والله ما قالوا هذا الكفار يقولون هؤلاء وهابية متعصبون وكلكم قرأتم أو سمعتم الصحافة الامريكية كثرة ما رددت تقول وهابيون متعصبون يعني نسبت الدعاة إلى ما في هذا البلد والدعوة والعقيدة الصحيحة والحمد لله وإن سموها هم وهابية هي عقيدة أهل السنة والجماعة وما جاء في الكتاب والسنة .

[Our enemies] have said: These [preachers] are not in [harmony] with the doctrine of the people of the Sunnah and Jama$^{c}$ah. Rather, they take th[at] doctrine as a means or method to [get] what they want. I seek refuge in God! The infidels ... the infidels, by God, [have] not [gone so far as to] say this. The infidels say: "These [preachers] are fanatic Wahabis." You all have read or heard the American press. How often has it repeated itself saying: "fanatic Wahabis!?" I mean, it has related the preachers to that which is of this country and to the *da$^{c}$wah* , and to the true doctrine, praise be to God. Even if they call it "Wahabism" it is the doctrine of the people of the Sunnah and Jama$^{c}$ah and that which has come [down to us] in [God's] Book and the Sunnah.

## Selection 15

عندما جاءت الفتنة يا إخوان — الازمة التي يسمونها أزمة الخليج
جاءت -- تكلم من تكلم منا وأبرأ ذمته . ولا أدل على أن الأمر هو إبراء
للذمة من اختلافنا نحن هؤلاء الذين يُذكر عنا -- الأربعة مثلاً الذين
ذكرت . كل واحد منا لو سمعتم تجد أخذ الموضوع من منحة خاصة .
ليش كل واحد يعبر عما يدين الله تعالى . صحيح أن الهدف واحد
والمؤد واحد والنصيحة لكن كل واحد يعبر . ليست كما ذكر هؤلاء أنها
أخطبوطات في الخفاء ولا .... هذا عبر وهذا عبر . أو كما اتهمونا انه
يعني يديرنا جهات خارجية . أعوذ بالله . نحن ندار من برة ؟
سبحان الله العظيم . والله نحن نعتبر أن هذا البلد بلد القيادة يا
إخوان . وهذا لا نقوله فخراً لا فخراً لكن حقيقة القيادة هنا . المنبع
هنا. ندار من الخارج ؟ يُملى علينا من برة ؟ قد يكون لنا إخوة في
الله يشاركوننا من أهل السنة في بعض أرائنا ومواقفنا طبيعة أهل
السنة أمة واحدة فرقة واحدة في كل مكان . لكن نحن نوجه من برة !؟
ندار من برة !؟

When the *fitnah* * came, O brothers -- the crisis which they call the "Gulf crisis" came -- each one of us who spoke [out], had his say and met his obligation. And, there is nothing more indicative [of the fact] that the matter is one of the meeting of an obligation than our own differing, those who are mentioned -- the four [of us] for instance, who have been mentioned. Each one of us, if you listen you'll find, has taken the issue [up] from a particular perspective. Why did each one give expression to that which God, may He be exalted, condemns? It is true that the aim was one, the task was one, [as was] the advice. But, each one of us gave [his own] expression [to it]. It is not as those [enemies of ours] have said: "[The Sheikhs' comments are] octopuses in hiding." Or ... this one expressed himself and the other expressed himself. [N]or is it as they charge us that, I mean that foreign agencies are directing us. I seek refuge in God! We are directed from abroad? Glory be to God Most Great! We, by God, consider this country to be the leading country O brothers. And, we do not say this out of pride. Not pride, but the reality of leadership is here. The well-spring is here. We are directed from abroad!? We are dictated to from abroad! We may have brothers in God who share [with] us -- among the people of the Sunnah -- some of our ideas and positions. [That is] the nature of the people of the Sunnah, one community, one group everywhere. But we are instructed from abroad? We are directed from abroad?

* The term فِتْنَة, which might be translated "civil strife" here, is a deeply emotive word. It is applied to the first civil wars among the Muslims which still bear heavily on Muslim historical consciousness. It also has meanings related to "seduction." It has the impact of English "bloodlust."

## Selection 16

أقول لكم عن ما أعرفه شخصياً . هؤلاء الذين كتبوا وطعنوا كانوا
يمدحون ويثنون عليّ بمالانا اعلم والله لفيه مبالغة . وأنا أقول لهم لا
تبالغوا بارك الله وهذا و و ... موجود ويشهد به المئات إن لم أقل
ألوف ممن يحضر مجالسهم حتى جاءت هذه الازمة ... لما جاءت الازمة
وكانٍ لنا رأي فيه نوع مخالفة أو معارضة للموقف الرسمي للدولة
إبراءً للذمة نحن ... لا في هذا البلد ... ما عندنا معارضة سياسية ...
معارضة حزبية . عندنا كلمة حق تقال . لا خير فينا إن لم نقلها ولا
خير فيهم إن لم يسمعوها . إن أخذوا بها فالحمد لله وإن لم يأخذوا بها
برأت ذمتنا . وهم الله تعالى حسيبهم . وقد يكون اجتهادهم هو
الصواب ونحن نقول ولا زلنا نقول إن هذا رأي . ما فيه وحي نزل من
السماء . رأي . لما قلنا هذا الكلام انقلبت المحبة والمبالغة في المدح إلى
عداوة مقيتة شديدة غريبة

I'll tell what I know about personally. Those who wrote and slandered had been praising and lauding me in [a way] that I know, by God, did have some exaggeration to it. I was saying to them: "Do not exaggerate, may God bless you." This happened, and hundreds, if I don't say "thousands," of those who attended their meetings [could] testify to that. Until the crisis came ... when the crisis came, and we had an opinion in which [there] was some kind of difference or opposition towards the official standpoint of the state, to meet our own obligation ....* [There is] not, in this country ... we do not have a political opposition ... a party opposition. We have righteous speech proclaimed. There is no "good" among us if we have not proclaimed [that speech]. And, there is no "good" among them [our opponents] if they do not listen to it. If they accept it, then praise be to God. If they do not accept it, we have [at least] fulfilled our obligation, and they, God will settle with them. Their *'ijtihad* might be right, but we say and have not ceased saying: "This is an opinion. It does not [contain] any revelation which has descended from heaven. An opinion." When we said that, the love and exaggerated praise changed into an odious, sharp, strange hostility.

* Sheikh Safar seems to lose his train of thought here.

## Selection 17

العلمانين فرحوا قالوا << هه ... مادام خالفوا الحكومة إذاً يريدون الحكم يريدون الكراسي يريدون المناصب يريدون مثل الترابي مثل غنوشي مثل عباس المدني >> وجاؤوا ب ... لا ... طيب ... في هذا الوقت بالذات -- وكتب القصيبي توزع وكلام الجرائد كل يوم إلا ما وفقه الله منها لا نعني الجميع طبعاً -- << تأتي الاشرطة وتوزع في وقت واحد . اذاً ماذا ؟ هل عقل مدبر واحد ؟ >>

The secularists rejoiced and said: "Huh! As long as the[ scholars] have disputed the Government, therefore they want to rule, they want the seats [of power], they want positions, and they want the like of what al-Turabi, Ghannushi, [and] CAbbas Al-Madani [want]."* The[se secularists] put out ...fine... no! At this exact time, al-Qusaibi's† books were being distributed, and the newspapers were talking everyday -- save those whom God had guided; we don't mean all [of them], of course -- [saying] "the tapes have come [out], and they are being distributed at the same time. So what is [this]? It there one organizing mind [behind the Islamist movement]?"

* Hasan al-Turabi, Rashad Ghannushi, and CAbbas al-Madani are the leaders of the major Islamist movements in, respectively, Sudan, Tunis and Algeria.

† Ghazi al-Qusaibi is a Saudi Arabian diplomat and author closely associated with the regime.

## Selection 18

واحد آخر بلغه -- خطأ طبعاً كذباً -- أن الشيخ سلمان العودة قد اعتقل فسجد سجود شكر والله نعم يا إخوان حصلت . نسأل الله العافية . أعوذ بالله ! ليش ؟ شوفو الضغينة . هذه ما هي مخالفة . لو كان -- كما يقولون -- خلاف فقهي طيب إذا بلغك أن الشافعي كلامه راجح ولا مالك مرجوح مثلاً تسجد ؟ علم و فقه لكن الدليل أنه هناك ضغينة وشئ آخر أكثر من قضية أنه والله أخطأ أو أصاب أو مجتهد أو غير مجتهد

[There was] another one who heard -- mistakenly of course (it was a lie) -- that Sheikh Salman al-ᶜAwdah had been arrested. So, he prostrated himself in a prayer of thanks, by God! Yes, O brothers. It happened! We ask God [for His] protection; I seek refuge in God. Why? [Just] look [at] the malice! This is not a "disagreement." If it were -- as they say [it is] -- a jurisprudential dispute, fine. If you heard that Shafiᶜi's* dictum was the more weighty or that Malek's† had been rejected, for example, would you prostrate yourself in prayer? [This] knowledge and jurisprudence, but the evidence is that there is malice and something other, and more, than an issue [of whether], by God, [someone] has made a mistake or been correct or is a *mujtahed* or not a *mujtahed*.

* The tenth century jurist who is credited with the most complete description of the Islamic legal system in its fullest flower.

† The eighth century jurist who laid out the first description of the emerging Islamic legal system.

### Selection 19

إذاً يعني ... شئ يعني ... ماسونية أو ايش ... بعبع رهيب لا حقيقة له . كل الدنيا تدار بهذا الشكل الوهمي . فهذه التوهمات التي ... يعني... هي ... مثل هذه وهم آخر توهموه -- معاداة العلماء ... إن هؤلاء يعادون العلماء... يعادون العلماء سبحان الله . نحن والحمد لله كل أربعة أسابيع نحن رابع ... كل رابع أسبوع نحن في اجتماع مع سماحة الشيخ والحمدلله . دائماً من بعد الأزمة هذه . ونحن والحمد لله كل رابع أسبوع -- وغير اللقاءت التي تقع أحياناً في يعني بعد أسبوعين أو أقل من ذلك غير الاتصالات غير المراسلات غير المشاورات في أمور الدعوة غير ما نعطيهم من قوائم تعطون إياها هنا ونرفعها لسماحته ... سماحة الشيخ محمد العثيمين حفظه الله . تعلمون والله يشهد على ذلك أيضاً حبنا وصلتنا له وفرحنا بمجيئه وكل العلماء

So, I mean [our enemies say it is] ... I mean ... a Masonic thing or whatever! A frightful scare tactic in which there is no truth. The world is directed by this delusional form [of conspiracy, they say]. These illusions which ... I mean ... are .... Like them is another illusion which they have dreamed up -- hostile feelings for the [senior] scholars ... these [your humble servants] are hostile towards the [senior] scholars, glory be to God! We, praise be to God, every four weeks we ...

the fourth ... every fourth week, we are in a meeting with his Eminence, the Sheikh. Praise be to God, [we] always [see him] after this crisis. And we, praise be to God, every fourth week -- aside from [our] meetings which occur, occasionally, at , I mean, within two weeks or less than that -- other than [our] contacts], other than [our] exchanges of messages, other than [our] consultations on *da$^{c}$wah* issues, other than the lists which we give them -- you give them [to us] here, and we bring them up to his Eminence, Sheikh Mohammed al-$^{c}$Uthaymin, may God preserve him. You know, and God is a witness to this as well, our love, our commitment to him, and our joy in his coming [to see us] a[s with] all scholars.

## Part 3

### "Attacks on Preachers" from *The Dregs of the Kuwaiti Press* by Salman al-[c]Awdah

#### Selection 1

أيها الاحبة إن الصحافة تفقد مصداقيتها حين تكون صحافة مجاملة همها التربيط على اكتاف الحكام والتصفيق للمعتدين — المعتدين على أعراض الناس وحرياتهم وممتلكاتهم وحقوقهم فالصحافة هي نفس الانسان ويفترض أن تكون تعبيراً حقيقياً عن مشاكله وهمومه وطموحاته وآماله وآلامه وتطلعاته أما أن تمارس الصحافة دورها بشكل مقلوب فهذه هي النكسة العظمى والاجحاف الكبير بحق الامة وهذا هو التنكر للرسالة التي كان يجب على الصحافة أن تحملها .إننا ننتظر من الصحافة بجميع مؤسساتها أن تكون مدافعاً شجاعاً عن مصالح المجتمع أن تكون منبراً حراً لصوت الحق وأن تكون أداة فعالة لبناء الامة بناءً عقائدياً يحفظ للامة استقلالها في وجه عواصف التغيرويمنحها الثقة بذاتها وتاريخها ومستقبلها وشخصيتها المستقلة وفي نفس الوقت ننتظر من الصحافة أن تكون مجالاً صالحاً للنقد البناء الهادف النزيه مهما كان هذا النقد مراً على النفوس فهذا هو العهد المأخوذ على خير القرون كما في حديث عبادة ابن الصامت رضي الله عنه . إنه قال فيما أخذ عليهم النبي صلى الله عليه وسلم وأن نقول بالحق حيثما كنا لانخاف في الله لومة لائم

O beloved, the press loses its credibility when it becomes a journalism of politeness whose [prime] concern is binding itself onto the shoulders of rulers and applauding aggressors -- aggressors against the people's honor, freedoms, property, and rights. The press is the [life's] breath of mankind. It ought to be a true expression of [mankinds'] problems, worries, aspirations, hopes, pains and expectations. As for the press practicing its role in a wrong way, well, this is [a] great setback, [a] huge injustice to the Community's due; this is [a] denial of the mission which the press must bear. We expect the press, with all it establishments, to be a brave defender of society's interests, to be a free pulpit for the voice of truth, to be an effective instrument to build the community faithfully, preserving the community's independence in the face of storms of change and granting it confidence in it's self, its history, its future and its independent personality. At the same time, we expect the press to be a suitable arena for constructive, well-aimed, pure criticism, however bitter this criticism may be to [our] souls. This is the charge taken up [by the press] through the best of centuries as [we learn] from the *hadith* from ᶜAbadah Ibn al-Samet, may God be pleased with him. He said, as regards that which the Prophet, may God bless him and grant him peace, enjoined upon them: "[Were] we to tell the truth, wherever we might be, we [would] not fear, in God, the blame of any censurer."

## Selection 2

أيها الإخوة إنه لايقرّب من أجل ولايباعد من رزق أن يتكلم هؤلاء المتربعون على عرش الصحافة عن الانتهاكات التي لاتنتهي لعقائد الناس والتي أصبحت تؤرق المسلم وتقلقه وتجعله يعيش في عناءً كبير حتى وهو في بلده وبين أهله وعشيرته . لقد أصبح الكثير من الناس يعتقدون أن الكافر يهودياً كان أونصرانياً أقرب إليهم وشيجةً ولحمةً من أخيهم المسلم وأن الاجنبي أقرب اليهم من أخيهم في النسب والعرق فأين حمية الاسلام إذاً وإذا لم تكن حمية الاسلام فأين نخوة العروبة التي كان ابوجهل وابولهب ينتخون بها ويتنادون إليها؟ أين الموقف الناضج من ذوبان الشخصية الاسلامية في شخصية المستعمر سواء كان هذا المستعمر أمريكياً أوبريطانيا حتى أصبحنا نجد المواطن العادي في أكثر من بلد قد يسمي ولده كما سمعتم وقرأتم بجورج بوش عبدالله والآخر يلبس قلادة عليها صورة ثاتشر

O brothers, [the fact] that those squatting on the thrones of the press [should] speak of violations of people's beliefs (which do not end and which [violations] have come to upset the Muslim, make him anxious and make him live in great concern -- even though he is in his [own] country and among his [own] people and family ) [that fact] does not bring the end any closer or push [God's] sustenance any further off. Many people have come to believe that the nonbeliever, whether Jewish or Christian, is closer to them, in flesh and [blood] relationship, than [is] their brother Muslim and that the foreigner is closer to them than their brother in flesh and [blood] lineage. Where, then, is protection for Islam? And, if the protection of Islam does not exist, then where is the dignity of Arabism for which Abu Jahl and Abu Lahab risked themselves and after which they strove?* Where is a mature position against the dissolution of the Islamic personality into the colonialist's personality whether this colonizer be American or British such that we find the ordinary citizen in many countries may name his child, as you've heard and read, "George Bush ᶜAbdullah" while another wears a necklace upon which is hung a picture of Thatcher.

* See Qur'an 111 for Abu Lahab, a byword for stubborn resistance to the Prophet Muhammad in favor of (pre-Islamic) Arab identity. So too Abu jahl though not mentioned in the Qur'an.

## Selection 3

أصبحنا نتنكر للجماعات الاسلامية في كل بلد إسلامي ونرميها بكل البذاءت وكل الالفاظ الشنيعة . وأقل مايمكن أن نقول لهم أنهم وقفوا مع صدام حسين ومع غزو العراق للكويت وأنهم انتهازيون وأنهم ذو أهداف مادية سياسية وأنه لايعنيهم أمر الإسلام إنما الإسلام بالنسبة لهم هو مجرد حصالة نقود أو مجرد ثوب يلبسونه صباحاً ليخلعونه مساء . أصبحنا نطلق هذه العبارات على كل الجماعات الإسلامية وعلى كل من يرفعون راية الدعوة إلى الإسلام في كل بلد . وهذا والله من الظلم الكبير . تنكرنا لعلماء الدين فأصبحنا نصفهم بكل نقيصة نصفهم بالجهل نصفهم بالتخلف نصفهم بالتطرف نصفهم بالعنف نصفهم بكل الألفاظ البذيئة التي نحفظها في قاموسنا وأخيراً تنكرنا لشباب البلاد أنفسهم فأصبحنا نصب عليهم جام غضبنا ومرير حقدنا ونستخدم ألفاظ البذاءة والسباب والشتائم لنسوّد بها صفحات جرائدنا ومجلاتنا وصحفنا في محاولة إلهاب السياط في ظهور هؤلاء الابرياء

We have begun to decry the Islamic groups in every Islamic country and to level at them every obscene and repugnant term. The least that we can say about them is that they stood with Saddam Husain and with Iraq's attack against Kuwait; that they are opportunists; that they have materialist and political goals, and that the matter of Islam does not concern them but rather that Islam is, for them, a mere means of obtaining money or a mere cloak which they put on in the morning and take off at night. We have begun to apply these phrases to all the Islamic groups and to all of those who raise the banner of the call to Islam in every country. This, by God, is a great injustice. We've decried the religious scholars. We've begun to describe them [as having] every fault; we describe them with [the term] "ignorance"; we describe them with [the term] "backwardness"; we describe them with [the term] "extremism"; we describe them with [the term] "violence"; we describe them by every obscene word we keep in our dictionaries, and finally, we've decried the youth of the country themselves. We've begun to spill onto them the cup of our anger and the bitterness of our hatred. We use the terms of obscenity, blasphemy and insults to blacken the pages of our newspapers, magazines and journals in an attempt to bring down* whips on the backs of these innocents.

* Lit. "to incite."

## Selection 4

لقد أصبح المثقف الان يقول انتهى عهد العنتريات العربية وجاء عهد التفكير المنطقي الواقعي البعيد عن التشنج . جاء عهد النظرة المعتدلة التي لاتنظر إلى العالم من منطلق العداء للعالم كله إنما منطلق المصالح المتبادلة . وحين تدخل إلى التفاصيل تجد أحدهم يقول تفسيراً للكلام السابق أنه قد آمن با لامبريالية وآمن بإعداء الاستعمار فهم الضمادة التي تلتف حول جروحنا وعملهم هو ترسيخ لمبادئ الحرية والكرامة والانسانية . ماذا لو طولب بمحاكمة مثل هؤلاء الناس بتهمة الولاء للاستعمار ، الاستعمار الذي يعلم الله كنا بالأمس نقرأ في كتب التاريخ أن هناك أناساً كانوا أعواناً للاستعمار في بلاد المشرق العربي الإسلامي .

The *cultured* [person] has now come to say: "the era of the Arab $^{c}$*Antariyyah* has ended and the era of logical, realistic thinking far from convolutions has come; come is the era of the moderate viewpoint which does not look at the world from a position of hostility towards the world as a whole but from a perspective of shared interests." When you get into details, you find one of them saying, as an explanation of the preceding statement, that he has believed in imperialism *and* he has believed in hostility to colonialism. [The juxtaposition of imperialism and anti-imperialism] are the dressings which bind up our [more ancient] wounds. The process [of the two] is [a necessary prelude to] the rooting of the principles of freedom, honor, and humanity [in our social soil]. What if condemning these people on a charge of loyalty to colonialism were demanded?! [This is] the colonialism [about] which, God knows, we were, [just] yesterday reading in history books that there were people who were agents of colonialism in the countries of the Arab-Islamic east.

## Selection 5

يوجد بيننا من يقول ما المانع من إقامة قواعد عسكرية لهم في بلادنا فنحن بحاجة إليهم ليدافعوا عنا كما نحن بحاجة إلى صناعتهم وتعميرهم لبلادنا المخربة إنها كارثة والله أن تذوب حواجز العقيدة مع هؤلاء ليقوم بدلها حواجز مع بني جلدتنا وأولاد أسرنا لمجرد أنهم كانوا متحمسين للإسلام أكثر منا

There are those who say: "What's the objection to setting up military bases for them in our country? We need them to protect us just as we are in need of their industry and construction in our destroyed country." It is a disaster, by God, that obstacles of doctrine regarding them should dissolve such that, in their place, obstacles against the sons of our [own] flesh and the children of our [own] families should arise for the mere fact that they were more zealous for Islam than we!

## Selection 6

وإنها لكارثة أكبر أن تصبح بديهيات الدين مجالاً للاخذ والرد والجدال فالبراءة من المشركين اليوم لاوجود لها في قاموس طائفة ممن يتسنمون على عروش الصحافه فقد ضاعت عندهم الاوراق واختلطت الحدود وضاعت المفاهيم فأصبح الكافر المشرك صديقاً لدوداً حبيباً . لماذ ؟ لانه وقف معهم فيما يزعمون ويدعون وأصبح الصديق المؤمن عدواً لانه في نظرهم يقاوم طغيان الغرب أو طغيان الشرق كما أصبح الكثيرون يشككون مثلاً في قضية العقوبات الإلهية التي ينزلها الله تعالى بمن يخالفون أمره

It is [an even] greater disaster that religion's truisms have become an arena for give-and-take and conflict. Avoiding polytheists today, there is no place for it in the dictionaries of the clique of those who mount the thrones of the press. They've lost their cards, and limits have gotten mixed up; understanding has been lost. So, the polytheistic infidel has become a friend -- a *beloved* foe. Why? Because he stood by them, as they claim and assert. The faithful friend has become an enemy because he, in their view, was resisting the West's oppression *and* the East's oppression. Similarly, many have come to doubt, for example, the matter of holy sanctions which God, may He be exalted, is bringing down on those who contravene His orders.*

* A reference to the UN sanctions against Iraq whose sarcasm is apparent in Sheikh's tone of voice. See the tape.

## Selection 7

وأصبحنا نجد حملة ضارية شرسة في عدد من الصحف على مجموعة
من الدعاة لمجرد أنهم قالوا إن ما نزل من البلاء والمصيبة كان بسبب
ذنوبنا ومعاصينا وهل هذا الامر يحتاج إلى إثبات بعد أن قال الله
تعالى لصفوة البشر بعد الرسل والانبياء لاصحاب محمد صلى الله
عليه وسلم وقد أصابهم ما أصابهم قال الله تعالى << أولما أصابتكم
مصيبة قد أصبتم مثليها قلتم إني هذا قل هو من عند أنفسكم >>

We've begun to find a savage, vicious campaign in a number of newspapers against a group of preachers for the mere [fact] that they said: "The disaster and catastrophe which has come down [upon us] was by reason of our sins and transgressions." Is this a matter which is in need of proof after God, may He be exalted, said to the choicest of men -- after the apostles and prophets -- [that is] to the Companions of Muhammad (may God bless him and grant him peace), after that which had afflicted them having afflicted them [in fact] ... God, may He be exalted, said: "Is it not the case that when a disaster -- twice the likes of which you caused -- struck you, you said: 'This is not of me!' Say [rather]: 'It is from within ourselves.'"*

* Qur'an 3:165.

## Selection 8

إن الكل مندهش من هذه الحملة الصحفية الكويتية خاصة على شباب
الدعوة الاسلامية ونحن لانخرج أحداً من الاسلام بذنب إلا الشرك بالله
تعالى اللهم إلا المكفرات المعروفة التي تكلم عنها أهل العلم وأقول هذا
لأن لايخرج علينا أحد في الغد أو بعد غد ويقول أنتم تكفروننا وأنتم
تخرجوننا من الاسلام ولكننا نعلم ويعلم الناس أن الشباب المستهدفين
بهذه الحملة الظالمة الاثمة هم عمار المساجد وهم أهل حلق الذكر وهم

طلاب العلم وهم حملة الدعوة وهم الملتزمون بالسلوك الاسلامي
المتحمسون لقضية الدعوة إلى الله تعالى أكثرمن غيرهم

Every one is astonished by this Kuwaiti journalistic campaign, especially [that part of it] against the youth of the Islamic *da*$^{c}$*wah*. We do not expel anyone from Islam for any sin except polytheism,* may God be with us, except for well-known profanities which the scholars† have spoken of. I say this so that no one may, tomorrow or the day after, come out and say: "You are calling us 'unbelievers,' and you are expelling us from Islam!" But, we know, and the people know, that the youth targeted by this unjust, sinful campaign are the mosque builders. They are the people of *dhikr* circles‡; they are seekers after knowledge; they carry [forward] the *da*$^{c}$*wah*; they are the ones committed to Islamic paths, to the issue of calling [people] unto God (may He be exalted) more than any others.

* Lit. "ascribing a partner to God" and hence "polytheism;" the major sin in Islamic theology.

† Lit. "people of science."

‡ "Circles" of people getting together to chant the name of God or verses of the Qur'an; usually associated with Sufi practice.

## Chapter Six

# The Aims of the West

## Introduction

Safar al-Hawali, in his lecture "The True Promise and the False One," identifies ten points of the program which he believes a hostile West has for the Islamic East. The anti-Semiticism in several passages cannot be excused, even as an expression of the outrage felt by those who deem themselves to be under mortal threat. Sheikh Safar's contemporary version of the ancient "Blood Libel" is especially repugnant.* It is, however, a reality which it would do us well to recognize.

* See "Selection 9" below.

## Chapter Six

**"Ten Points and More"** from ***The True Promise and the False One*** by **Safar al-Hawali**

### Selection 0

بقيت قضية مهمة لابد أن نأتي عليها . وهي تتكون من شقين . الشق الاول ما هي النتائج المتوقعة لما يسمّى مشروع السلام الحالي وبالتالي ماذا يراد بهذه المنطقة عندما تُدفع إلى الايمان بالوعد المفترى وتكفر بالوعد الحق من الله تبارك وتعالى؟ أقول لاخواني الكرام إن الاهداف كثيرة والنتائج خطيرة وأرجو ألا تستغرقنا جزئيات وتفاصيل الاحداث فننسى هذه الاهداف البعيدة وأرجو أن لا تعتبروا ما سأقوله لكم أنه كل الاهداف فهناك ما هو أكثر من ذلك وإنما إشارات جُمعت من خلال الوقائع والبيانات التي يُصدرها هؤلاء في كتبهم قديما وحديثاً

One important issue has been left to which we must come. It consists of two parts. The first part is: what are the results [to be] expected from what is called the current "Peace Plan." And subsequently, what is desired of this region when it is pushed into belief in the "False Promise" and has forsworn the "True Promise from God," may He be glorified and exalted? I say to my noble brothers: "The aims are many, and the results are dangerous." I hope that particularities and the details of events will not so engross us that we forget about these long range goals. I hope that you don't consider what I am going to say to be all the[ir] goals because there are more than [just] these. [These] rather are [only] indications which have been collected from documents and statements which these [enemies of ours] have issued in their books, both in the past and recently.

### Selection 1

أولاً يريدون القضاء على الجهاد الفلسطيني داخل الارض المحتلة الذي يسمّى الانتفاضة . بعد السلام لا يعود المجاهدون الفلسطينيون لا يعودون محتلين يدافعون عن بلادهم وإنما يتحولون تلقائيا إلى مواطنين يحاربون دولتهم . وبالتالي فلا شرعية لأي عمل يعملونه فمن حق أي دولة أن تقمع رعاياها إذا خرجوا على قانونها كما يقرر في القانون الدولي . وهذا هدف كبير لأن أخطر ما تخاف إسرائيل منها

الآن هو هؤلاء . يعني الدول العربية من زمان رفعت يدها عن القضية. ولا تطمع إسرائيل ولا تحلم بأن العرب سيحاربونها لكن الخوف من هذا الوعي الإسلامي المتنامي داخل الارض المحتلة هذه واحدة

First, they want to put an end to the Palestinian *jihad* in the occupied territory which is called the "*Intifadha*." After "Peace," the Palestinian *mujahidin* will no longer ... they will no longer be [the] colonized defending their country. Rather, they will be automatically transformed into citizens battling their [own] government, and thereafter there will be no legality to any action which they carry out. It is the right of any state to restrain its subjects if they violate its law, as is stated in International Law. This is a major goal because that which Israel now most fears is these [mujahidin]. I mean, the Arab states long ago abandoned [this] issue. Israel does not want, and does not dream that, the Arab states will fight it, but the[ir] fear is of this growing Islamic sentiment inside the occupied territory. This is one [of their aims].

## Selection 2

ثانيا يريدون بهذا السلام العام بين العرب واليهود التضييق على الدعوة الاسلامية وضرب الحركة الاسلامية في كل مكان قد تُضرب ربما ضربات مباشرة وقوية في كل مكان من المغرب إلى إندونيسيا كما عبر نكسون . يريدون أن يستفيدوا من هذا لضرب هذه الدعوة وسمعتم ماذا قال ماذا قرر مجلس الامن القومي الامريكي .

Secondly, they want, by this general peace [accord] between the Arabs and the Jews, to restrict Islamic proselytizing and to strike the Islamic movement everywhere it may be struck, perhaps direct, strong blows everywhere from Morocco to Indonesia as Nixon stated. They want to take advantage of this ["peace" accord] to strike the *da'wah*. You have heard what the American Security Council decided.

## Selection 3

ثالثا تدمير القوى العربية المحيطة بإسرائيل رغم أنها قد لا تشكل خطراً عليهم . العراق دُمّر وسوف تكون الخطوة التالية تدمير الجيش السوري . ليس خوفا من حافظ الاسد والعصابة النصيرية فإنهم لم

يكونوا يخافون أيضا من العصابة البعثية في بغداد ولكن لأن الجيش السوري لديه قوة و لديه نوع من التدريب . ولديه شئ من الممارسة والخبرة . فقد يشكل خطراً ما على اليهود فيما لو سقطت هذه الحكومة وقامت حركة إسلامية وأعلنت الجهاد وانضم إليها جيش مدرب ومجهز و شارك في بعض حروب وشارك في لبنان . فلديه نوع من الخبرة العسكرية . فلابد من تدمير الجيش البعثي السوري . وعندها يقول البعثيون في سورية « أكلت يوم أكل الثور الابيض »

Thirdly, to destroy the Arab powers surrounding Israel, even though they do not represent a danger to them. Iraq has been destroyed, and the next step will be the destruction of the Syrian Army -- not out of fear of Hafiz al-Asad and the Nusayri gang* (nor have they been afraid of the Ba'thi gang in Baghdad†) -- but because the Syrian army has the power of some kind of training. It has some bit of practice and experience. So, it might form some kind of a threat to the Jews were this government [of Asad's] to fall and an Islamic movement to arise and declare *jihad* and [were] a trained and ready army -- and [one] which has participated in several wars and in Lebanon -- to align itself with [that Islamic movement]. For, it does have some sort of military experience. So, the Syrian, Ba'thi army must be destroyed. Then the Ba'thists in Syria will say, "I was eaten on the day the white ox was eaten."‡

* Nominally, the Syrian regime adheres to the secularist "Syrian Socialist Resurrectionist (Ba^c thi) Party." The central prop of, and constituency for, Hafiz al-Asad's regime, however, is a Syrian Shi^c ite sect or community usually referred to as the ^c Alwis or ^c Alawites. Here Sheikh Safar applies an alternative designation to that community, further denigrating it by the perjorative "gang."

† Here the reference is to the "Iraqi Socialist Resurrectionist Party," a branch of the party in competition with that of Syria mentioned above.

‡ I have not found reference to this phrase, which appears to be a proverb.

## Selection 4

رابعا إخضاع المنطقة للرهبة اليهودية العسكرية وفرض الحماية
الامريكية على المنطقة ومنع -- كما أعلنوا -- منع تطوير أي جيش من
جيوش المنطقة . وإنما يراد بقاء الجيوش للمحافظة على الامن الداخلي
فقط لأنه في ظل النظام الدولي الجديد ما الحاجة إلى أن تطور جيشاً ؟
أتريد أن تستخدمه في العدوان كما فعل صدام ؟ لا . إذاً ماذا تريد ؟
تريد الامن والحدود ؟ النظام الدولي يكفل لك الامن والحدود . تريد
الامن الداخلي ؟ نعم ! فلتكن قوات فقط للامن الداخلي . ولا تفكر في
أي حالة عداء مع الجيران . هذا هو الهدف الذي من أجله خططوا
ولسيناريو حرب الخليج واحتلال الكويت . وبثوا وأصلوا حتى أصبح
قاعدة راسخة عند شعوب المنطقة .

Fourth, to subjugate the region to Jewish, military terror, to impose [an] American protectorate on the region, and to prevent -- as they have announced -- to prevent the development of any one of the region's armies. The maintenance of armies is desired to preserve internal security only. Because, under the auspices of the "New World Order," what need is there for you to develop an army? Do you want to use it for aggression as Saddam did? No! Then what do you want? You want security and [safe] borders? The international regime will provide you [with] security and [stable] borders. Do you want internal security? Yes! Then let there be a few forces for internal security only. Don't, in any circumstance, think of hostility against [a] neighbor. This is the goal, for the sake of which they plotted, and the Gulf War scenario, and the invasion of Kuwait. And, they propagandized and planted [it] until it became a deep-rooted principle with the people of the region.

## Selection 5

خامسا -- و هو خطير جدا -- تغير المناهج الاعلامية والتعليمية لمحو
كل ما يثير العداء نحو اليهود . وهذا أعلنه شمير في المؤتمر . قال <<
لابد من تغيير ثقافاتكم >> << لابد من تغيير ثقافتكم العدائية نحو
اليهود>> -- المناهج الاعلامية والتعليمية كل شئ . يعني << العدو
الاسرائيلي>> ما عاد نسمعها . << دويلة الكيانات >> << الكيان
الصهيوني>> انتهت . << العصابات >> انتهت . الآن << دولة >> و << لها

حق العيش >> و <<عاصمتها -- يعني-- القدس >> . وكل شئ سيتم ولو على مراحل . فتنتهي كل الشعارات . ينتهي حتى كل ما يثير العداء دينيا . وقد عُمل بهذا في مصر . وغُيّرت المناهج تغييرا فظيعا جدا . حُذفت معارك اليهود مع النبي صلى الله عليه وسلم . حُذفت الاشارات إلى عداواتهم للنبي صلى الله عليه وسلم من مناهج التعليم. حُذفت كل الدلائل التي تؤدي ولو بالاستشمام إلى أن اليهود أعداء للمسلمين . حتى بعض الشيوخ الذين علاقاتهم حسنة بالانظمة وباركوا خطواتها -- باركوا خطوات السادات -- يعني ما عندهم أي اعتراض . المسألة عندهم عادية جدا . لما جاءوا في تفسيرهم إلى أيات اليهود يحذفونها . لو تتبعتم تفاسيرهم في التلفزيون يفسرون الايات فإذا جاء إلى أيات فيها اليهود يقطعونها وينتقلون إلى ما بعدها . هذا هو الذي يريدون أن يكون والعياذ بالله في المنطقة عموما . وكذلك في مناهج التعليم ... تُغير كل القضية التي ... وإن كانت مع الاسف كانت تُدرّس ... دُرّست لنا قضية قومية -- العرب واليهود وعد بلفور ومؤتمر سان ريمو و مؤتمر أنشاص . كله الكلام الفاضي اللي قريناه . ما فيه شئ إسلامي أبدا . بينما عشرين ألف مدرسة في أمريكا تدرس القضية على أنها قضية دينية توراتية فكيف بعد التغيير ؟

Fifthly, and this is very dangerous, to change media and educational programs so as to abolish everything that [might] provoke hostility toward the Jews. Shamir announced this at the conference. He said: "Your culture must change." "Your culture hostile to Jews must change" -- media and educational programs, everything. That means we'll no longer hear [the phrase]: "the Israeli enemy." [The terms] "a mini-state of creatures" and "the Zionist entity" [will be] finished! [The word] "gangs," done for! Now, [we'll have to say] "state" and "it has a right to exist." "Its capital is -- I mean -- Jerusalem!" Everything will come to an end even if in stages. All the slogans will be ended! Even anything which [could] provoke religious hostility. This has been done in Egypt. Curricula have been scandalously changed. The Jews' battles with the Prophet, may God bless him and grant him peace, have been omitted. References to their aggressions against the Prophet, may God bless him and grant him peace, have been omitted from education programs! All indications that [could] lead, even by implication, to [the idea] that the Jews are enemies of Muslims have been omitted! Even some sheikhs, whose relations with the [Arab] regimes are good and who have blessed their steps -- who blessed Sadat's steps I mean, make no objection! The problem is, for them, very simple. When they come, in their Qur'anic exegesis, to verses on the Jews, they omit them. If you follow their explications of the Qur'an on TV, they'll be interpreting verses and if they come to verses in which there are any Jews, they cut them out and move on to what [comes] after. That is what they want to be [true], all refuge is in God [alone], for the region in general. The same is [true] of educational curricula. The whole issue is changed which... even if it was, unfortunately, taught ... it has been taught to us as a nationalist issue -- the Arabs and the Jews; the Balfour Declaration, the San Remo Conference, and the Anshas* Conference. All of it is the empty words which we've studied. There is not a thing Islamic in it whatsoever. All the while twenty thousand schools in America are studying the issue as a religious, Torah one. So how should it be after the change?

* A city in Egypt

## Selection 6

سادسا فرض السيطرة المالية الاقتصادية اليهودية على المنطقة كلها .
ماذا يساوي اقتصادنا بالنسبة لاقتصاد الغرب؟ ماذا يساوي ؟ لا شئ !
الغرب سيطر اليهود عليه عن طريق الربا والبنوك الربوية . فكيف
إذا ملّكوا المنطقة هنا سوف يتحكمون في سنوات معدودات في كل
المال والاقتصاد في دول المنطقة جميعاً

Sixthly, to impose Jewish, financial, economic control on the whole region. What does our economy equate to with regard to the economy of the West? What does it equate to? Nothing! The West, the Jews have come to control it through usury and interest-bearing banks. So, how ... if they come to own the region, here, they will control, within a few years, all the property and economy of the states of the region, totally.

## Selection 7

سابعا اجتياح المنطقة بالثقافة اليهودية والنصرانية . ويصحب ذلك حملات تنصيرية . وقد رفع النصارى رؤوسهم وبدأوا يقولون إن أحداث الخليج هيأت لنا الفرصة لادخال دين المسيح في مناطق لم نكن نحلم أن ندخلها فيها من قبل . والتنصير يا إخوان علني والكنائس علنية ومؤيدة علنا في الكويت في الامارات في البحرين وموجود بشكل كثيف أيضا تنصير خبيث في اليمن وفي عُمان والاردن . الاردن مندوبها في مؤتمر مدريد نصراني وفيها تخطيط تنصيري رهيب . إذاً كلنا الآن كل البلاد محاطة بالتنصير فالبلد الذي يريدون أن ينصروه والعياذ بالله ولن يكون ذلك إن شاء الله هو هذه البلاد وسيعملون على ذلك قاتلهم الله . كما أننا نتوقع حملات تشويه ضد الاسلام تشويه للاسلام في كل المستويات لانهم يملكون هذا الاعلام الضخم الهائل وسوف تُعينهم الصحافة العربية ووسائل الاعلام العربية تعينهم على هذاَ الهدف عن طريق تشويه الدعاة وتشويه التاريخ الاسلامي كل هذا وارد ومتوقع وإن كان قد يأتي بنوع من البطؤ .

Seventh, to subdue the region through Jewish and Christian culture. Christian missionary campaigns will accompany that. The Christians have became optimistic and started to say: "The events of the Gulf have opened, for us, an opportunity to introduce the religion of the Messiah to regions which we never dreamt we [might] enter before. Th[is] Christian evangelism, O brothers, is open; the churches are public and openly supported in Kuwait, in the [United Arab] Emirates, in Bahrain. There is, in intensive form, an ugly Christian evangelism in Yemen, and in Oman and in Jordan. [As for] Jordan, its representative at the Madrid Conference is a Christian, and there is a terrible Christianizing plan there. Therefore, all of us, now, all the countries are surrounded by Christian evangelism. And, the country they want to Christianize, and [all] refuge is in God -- and it will never happen, God willing -- is *this* country. They are working for this, may God combat them. Similarly, we are expecting campaigns of slander against Islam, slander against Islam at all levels because they have this great, huge information [network]. The Arab press and the Arab information media will help them. It will help towards this goal by reviling [Islamic] preachers and [by] slandering the history of Islam. All this is approaching and to be expected, even though it might come somewhat gradually.

## Selection 8

ثامنا نهب ثروات المنطقة النفطية والمائية وتسخيرها لليهود ولامريكا . أما النفط فقد انتهوا منه تقريباً يعني هم قالوا لابد من حربين حرب النفط والثانية حرب المياه . حرب النفط انتهوا منها . الحرب الاخرى حرب المياه . يريدون أن ينتزعوا مياه الفرات ومياه العاصي ومياه الليطاني ومياه نهر الاردن وحتى النيل يمدوه بشبكات مائية يمدون من تحت القناة فيسحبون النيل سحباً إلى أرض فلسطين . وحتى المياه الجوفية في شمال المملكة شمال الجزيرة يريدون أيضا أن يسحبوها إلى داخل أرض فلسطين لبناء المستوطنات . ولذلك يقولون إن الحرب القادمة قد تكون حرب مياه . قد تُفتعل معركة أو خلاف بين تركيا وبين سوريا مثلا والعراق وهكذا . تدخل القضية فيضطر الامريكان للتدخل عسكريا فتنحل مشكلة الجيش السوري من جهة ومشكلة المياه من جهة أخرى لأن تركيا عضو في حلف الناتو . واليوم هذا الآن يجتمعون الغرب يجتمع أمس واليوم من أجل أن يضموا دول شرقية كثيرة إلى حلف الناتو لتطويره وتقويته . طيب ضد من يتقوون؟ اليوم بوش في لهاي من أجل هذا الموضوع . طيب لمن؟ ضد من تتقوون؟ وقد انتهى المعسكر الشرقي؟ يريدون ضم دول المعسكر الشرقي إلى الغربي لمقاومة العدو المشترك الذي لن يكون بطبيعة الحال إلا نحن . والحرب المائية كثير ما قيل أنها قادمة .

Eighth, to plunder the oil and water wealth of the region and subject it to the Jews and to America. As for oil, they've finished with it, almost. I mean, they've said: "There must be two wars: the oil war, and the second will be the water war." They've finished with the oil war. The other war is the water war. They want to snatch the waters of the Euphrates, the waters of the Assi, the waters of the Litani, the waters of the Jordan River and even the Nile. They [want to] send it through water networks which they w[ould] put under the canal, and draw the Nile into the land of Palestine. Even the underground waters in the north of the Kingdom, the north of the [Arabian] Peninsula, they also want to siphon it into the land of Palestine to build settlements. Therefore, they say: "The next war may be a water war." A conflict or dispute might be instigated between Turkey and Syria, for example, and Iraq and so on. The issue would start and the Americans would be compelled to intervene militarily. The Syrian Army problem, on the one hand, and the water problem, on the other, would be solved because

Turkey is a member of NATO. Today, just now, the West is holding a meeting -- it's been meeting yesterday and today -- about many eastern countries joining NATO to develop and strengthen it. Fine, against whom are they to become more powerful? Today, Bush is in the Hague about this subject. Fine, against whom? Against whom do they want to strengthen themselves? Having already finished with the Eastern camp? They want to include the states of the Eastern camp in the West to confront the common enemy which, naturally, will not be anyone but us. The water war, much is being said to the effect that it's coming.

## Selection 9

تاسعا إفساد المنطقة أخلاقيا . وهكذا طبع اليهود إذا دخلوا في أي بلد
عن طريق السياحة والاثار . سوف يفسدون المنطقة كلها — يعني دول
المنطقة جميعا — بالمخدرات وبالدعارة بالافلام القذرة المجلات القذرة –
– كل قذارة اليهود سوف يعممونها في المنطقة . وقد نشرت جرائدنا
نحن هنا وغيرها من جرائد كيف أرسلت إسرائيل عصابات من فتيات
حاملات لوباء الايدز إلى مصر لأنها مركز الثقل والقوة في العالم
الاسلامي . فسوف يعمم هذا على جميع البلاد والعياذ بالله .

Ninth, to corrupt the region morally. This is the nature of the Jews when they enter any country through tourism and archeology. They will corrupt the whole region -- that means all the states in the region -- through drugs, immorality, filthy films, filthy magazines -- all the dirt of the Jews, they will spread it throughout the region. Our newspapers, here -- and other newspapers, have published how Israel has sent groups of girls infected with the AIDS plague to Egypt because it is the center of influence and power in the Islamic world.* It will do the same to all countries. [The only] refuge is in God!

* This allegation is well known and reiterated in the Arab press fairly often; it is reminiscent of suspicions among elements of the African-American community that AIDS is being spread there by the American government. Actual incidents such as the "Tuskegee experiments" exacerbate the belief.

## Selection 10

عاشرا سوف يفتح الباب لغزو الجاسوسية اليهودية لأماكن ما كانت تحلم بها من قبل . وهذا هدف مهم جداً لأن إسرائيل تخطط بمقدار ما تتجسس على المنطقة وتعرف حقائقها فسوف يصلون إلى معرفة دقيقة عن الصحوة الإسلامية عن أعدائهم الحقيقيين عن حالة الجيوش وإن كان قد لا يخفى عليهم شئ لكن زيادة في الفن الاستخباراتي الذي يريده الإسرائيليون . هناك أيضا شئ متوقع أن يقع وهو اكتشاف الآثار اليهودية القديمة . عندهم ... أضرب لكم مثال على ذلك . تذكرون الدكتور هذا الصليبي الخبيث الذي طلع في لبنان ؟ الذي يقول إن الأرض التي خرج منها اليهود ليست مصر وإنما هي جنوب المملكة العربية السعودية ؟ وجاء بقرى ومناطق حول أبها؟ وقال تنطبق أسماء التوراة على هذه القرى ؟ وذكر .. يعني كلام عجيب . وردّ عليه حامد الجاسر وغيره . المهم عندهم شعور بأن هذه هي الأرض القديمة الملك الذي حفر الأخاديد أصحاب الأخدود كان يهوديا أيضا . إذاً هناك لهم آثار كما يزعمون خيبر المدينة مهد الذهب . يقولون إنه منجم سليمان عليه السلام كان يأخذ ذهب من مهد الذهب وغيرها . إذاً كل هذه مناطق سيقولون آثارنا سنبحث عنها ونحييها وننقب عنها . وهذا تمهيد للقول بأن هذه الأرض هي أرضنا قاتلهم الله وما يوفقون

Tenth, the gates will open before a Jewish espionage invasion into places they had not dreamed of before. This is a very important goal because Israel is planning the extent to which it might spy on the region and find out its actualities. They w[ant to] obtain a precise knowledge of the Islamic Awakening, of their real enemies, of the condition of Armies, even though nothing may be hidden from them but just to improve the intelligence technique[s] which the Israelis want. There is also a[nother] thing expected to happen. It is the discovery of ancient Jewish artifacts. They have ... I will give you an example of that. Do you remember this vile Crusader doctor who popped up in Lebanon? The one who said that the land from which the Jews departed is not Egypt but rather the south of the Kingdom of Saudi Arabia? He came up with names of towns and regions around Abha? He said [that] names in the Torah correspond with these towns? He stated ..., I mean strange talk! Hamed Al-Jaser and others have rebutted him. The important thing is that they have a feeling that *this* is th[eir] ancient land. The king who made the excavations, the people of the excavation, were also

Jews. Therefore, they have artifacts, as they claim: Khaybar, al-Madina, Mahd al-Dhahab. They say: "It is Solomon's mine, may peace be upon him. He used to take gold out of Mahd al-Dhahab and elsewhere. Therefore, these regions (they will say) [have] our artifacts; we're going to search for them, bring them to light and examine them." This is in preparation for saying:" This land is ours." May God combat them and they not be granted success.

# Chapter Seven

# What is to be Done ?

## Introduction

In two of the tapes, "A Condemnation of Celebrating the Unbelievers' Holidays" and "The True Promise and the False One," Sheikh Safar al-Hawali offers quite lengthy and specific programs as to how Muslims should respond to the unacceptable circumstances in which they find themselves. Given the West's present preoccupation with "Islamic Rage," as Robin Wright has called it, the central point to be sure to observe is that nowhere does Sheikh Safar justify, much less call for, violence despite his obviously heartfelt distress at the threat which he sees directed against Arabs and Islam and despite the horror he feels at the violence to which Muslims are subjected from North America through Europe, to North Africa and the Balkans, to India and beyond.

## Chapter Seven

### Part 1

### "Some Suggestions for a Response" from *A Condemnation of Celebrating Unbelievers' Holidays* by Safar al-Hawali

## Selection 1

ولعلكم تسألون — قبل أن أجيبكم على الاسئلة — عن الحلول . ما هي
الحلول التي يمكن أن نتخذها لدرء ومنع هذا المنكر الكبير ؟ أولا
الكلمة . لا تنسوا أهمية الكلمة ولا تنسوا قوة الكلمة وأن الله تبارك
وتعالى بعث رسله الكرام يدعون الناس بالكلام بالبلاغة بالنذارة .
ثم بعد ذلك يكون منهم الجهاد لكن الكلمة هي الاساس . فنحن ما بين
خطيب وواعظ ومدرّس ومتحدّث وإن لم يكن كذلك فهو في عمله
يستطيع أن يتحدّث . فيجب على الاخوة الخطباء أن يخطبوا الجمع
بهذا الشأن . وما بقي إلا تقريبا ثلاثة جمع ثم يأتي ... تأتي هذه
المواسم والاعياد الكفرية . الخطب إذاً مهمة جداً والحمد لله وصلاة
الجمعة يحضرها عامة الناس يعني نحن لو نظرنا إلى الحضور في هذه
المحاضرة التي نسأل الله أن يتقبل منا ومنكم إياها ويجعلنا جميعا
مجتمعين على ذكره وطاعته نحن طلاب علم في الغالب لكن الجمعة في
هذا المسجد وحده يجتمع مثل هذا العدد تقريبا مثلا وغيره من جميع
الناس من كل الفئات .

Perhaps you would like to ask, before I answer your questions, about solutions. What are the solutions which we can take to avert and prevent this great sin? First, "the word"! Don't forget the importance of "the word"; don't forget the power of the word and that God, may He be blessed and exalted, sent [His] honorable messengers to preach to people by the word, by rhetoric, by warning. Then, after that, there is among [those solutions] *jihad*, * but the word is the foundation. So, we are preachers, lecturers, teachers, and Hadith-scholars, and if [anyone] is not one of those, he (while at his work) can talk. [Our] brother preachers must preach [on] Fridays about this matter. Only about three Fridays remain and then it comes. These seasons and the infidel holidays come. Sermons are, therefore, very important. Praise be to God. And, Friday prayer, ... the public attends [Friday prayers]. That means, if we look at the attendance at this lecture -- which we ask that God accept from us (and from you) and [ask] that

He make us all united in calling out to Him and in obedience to him -- we are seekers of knowledge, for the most part, but Friday -- in this mosque, alone, a similar number, approximately, will gather, for instance -- and others of the whole people -- from all classes.

* Recall that the term جهاد means any action on behalf of religion and not especially "holy war."

## Selection 2

فلابد من إقامة الحجة عليهم بهذه الادلة وبما يفتح الله عليكم من غيرها
فلا يخفاكم ذلك . إذاً خطب الجمعة يكون فيها ذلك . وكذلك المواعظ
التي تكون ويقوم بها الاخوة بل يجب أن نقوم بها هذه الايام ونتجول
في المساجد ونحذّر الناس من ذلك . الآن وصلتنا أخبار — هذه
موجودة هنا — أن بعض المستشفيات قد علقوا « عيد سعيد »
وبدأوا يوزعون الكروت . والاسبوع الماضي أيضا جاءتنا . فإذاً هم قد
بدأوا يعملون ويشتغلون أهل المنكر وأهل الفساد فلابد أن يعمل أهل
الخير وأهل الاصلاح من الآن في المواعظ هذه . من ذلك أيضا نشر
المحاضرات والفتاوى والاحكام المتعلقة بهذه القضية — بهذا العيد .
ومن ذلك فتوى سماحة الشيخ الوالد محمد بن صالح العثيمين حفظه
الله هذه . موجودة عند الجميع أو تستطيعون الحصول عليها . ما
تعرفونها ؟ موجودة . طيب الحمد لله ... في مكتب التوعية موجودة .
ونرجو من الاخوان إن شاء الله أن كل مندوب حي يأخذ منها صوراً
ويوزّع ولو عشرة في كل مسجد ثم كل واحد منكم إذا أخذ نسخة
وقرأها يصوّر عشرة ... أو ثمان ... ثمان بريال خلوه ريال إن شاء الله
أنتم أكرم من ذلك بكثير خليه ريال لدرء هذا المنكر الكبير فتجد هذا
الريال بإذن الله تعالى خيراً عظيماً عند الله — إلى سبعمائة ضعف
في ميزانك — يوم القيامة .

So, the proof must be set out before them through these pieces of evidence and through such other means as God may make available to you. Th[ose other means] will not be hidden from you. Therefore, Friday sermons ... such [things should] be in them. Similar are th[ose] "exhortations"* which are .. which [our] brothers undertake to give. Indeed we must undertake to give them in these [upcoming] days, and [we must] go around to the mosques and warn people about that. Just now, information has reached us -- this [information] is to be found here -- that certain hospitals have hung up "Merry Christmas" [signs] and begun distributing cards. And, last week, as well, [such information] reached us. Therefore, the people of sin and the people of corruption have begun to act and work, so the people of good and the people of reform must act, as of now, through these exhortations. Some [other ways] of [doing] that, as well, are distributing lectures, *fatwas* and rulings relating to this issue -- [relating] to this holiday. Among those is this -- His Excellency Sheikh al-Waled Muhammed Ibn Salah al-$^{C}$Uthaymin's *fatwa* , may God preserve him. Everyone has it, or you can obtain it. You don't know it...? It is available ...? Fine .... Praise be to God ... in the Consciousness Raising Office ... it is to be found. We ask of the brothers, if God wills, that each neighborhood representative take a few copies of it and distribute [it] -- even if it be only ten -- in all the mosques. Then each one of you -- when he's taken a copy and read it -- [should] make ten ... or eight [copies] ... eight for a *riyal*. Let it be a *riyal*. If God wills, you'll be much more generous than that. Let it be one *riyal* to prevent this great sin. You will find, with the permission of God (may He be exalted), a great good before God -- as much as seven hundred times to your credit -- on the day of Judgment.

* The term مَوْعظة (plural مَواعظ) here rendered "exhortation" refers to a particular type of sermon-like religious discourse usually given at times other than the Friday noon prayer and outside of the mosque.

## Selection 3

ننشر هذه الفتوى . من أراد زيادة في الفتاوى ففتاوى اللجنة الدائمة
للإفتاء التي يرأسها سماحة الشيخ عبد العزيز بن باز حفظه الله
فتوى رقم ٢٥٤٠ والفتوى رقم ٣٣٢٦ والفتوى رقم ٩٢٥٤ والفتوى رقم
٨٨٤٨ وإن كانت موجزة لكنها صريحة وهي موجودة . من حصل منكم
على كتاب فتاوى اللجنة الذي طبع ... خرج مؤخراً فهي موجودة في
الجزء الاول من صفحة ٤٨ فما بعدها. تنشر وتوزع وتعلق في المساجد
وهذا أحد الوسائل .

Let us distribute this *fatwa* . Whoever has wanted more on *fatwas, fatwas* [come] from "The Permanent Committee on *Ifta'* " which His Excellency Sheikh Abdul-$^{C}$Aziz Ibn Baz, may God preserve him, heads. *Fatwa*s number 2540, 3326, 9254 and 8848, even though they are brief, nonetheless are clear and available. Whoever among you obtains the Committee's book of *fatwa*s, which was printed ... came out ... recently, they are found in the first volume from page 48 and thereafter. [These *fatwa*s should] be published, distributed, and posted in the Mosques. This is one means [of combatting the corruption of society through participation in unbelievers' holidays].

## Selection 4

من ذلك أيضا التوعية في المدارس . في الغالب إننا في حقل التعليم أو كثير من الاخوان في حقل التعليم . المدارس وسيلة مهمة جداً لنشر هذا الوعي . والطفل أو الطالب سوف يبلغ ذلك ويلزم يقال له ذلك . أن يبلغه أيضا لاهله ولجيرانه ولمن يستطيع . وهذا إن شاء الله في الامكان بإذن الله تعالى .

Among th[ose means], too, is "consciousness raising" in schools. For the most [part it] is [true] that we are in the field of education, or many of [our] brothers are in the education field. The schools are a very important means for spreading this awareness. The child, or the "student," will pass on this [consciousness], and this must be said to him -- that he also pass on [the word] to his family, to his neighbors and to whomever he can. This is, if God so wills, possible with God's permission; may he be exalted.

## Selection 5

يجب أن تعلق هذه الفتاوى مترجمة في الشركات التي يكون فيها كفار. وفتوى الشيخ العثيمين مترجمة ... موجودة .... وصلت ؟ جميل ! هذا هو مترجمة الحمد لله . إذاً موجودة مترجمة . إذاً تعلق في الشركات وفي المؤسسات . ولا يُكتفى بهذا بل يعلق ... هذه موجودة في مكتب التوعية اللي ما عنده يا إخوان ... بل تعلق الأوامر ... الأوامر الحكومية التي تمنع القيام بمثل هذه الاحتفالات . بل لا نكتفي بذلك . نطالب بأوامر جديدة . نطالب المسؤولين هذه الأيام بأوامر جديدة . وتترجم وتعلق وتختم في جميع الإدارات وفي جميع الشركات . وقد يكون من الحضور من هو مسؤل أو نحن يجب أن نبلغهم كل منا من طريقه أن هذا لابد منه . ومن يعملون في هذه الشركات الواجب عليهم أكثر أن يخاطبوا المسؤولين ويكتبوا بالطرق ... القنوات الرسمية المعروفة ويطلبوا التعاميم السابقة إن لم تكن

موجودة أو تعاميم جديدة تنهى عن هذا وتترجم بحسب لغة القوم يعني عندنا كفار والعياذ بالله من جميع الأجناس . فما يقول لك أنا الماني ولاّ إنجليزي ولاّ فرنسي ما أعرف إنجليزي . تترجم ما استطعنا بحسب الشركات وتعلق على أبواب ومكان أي مكان بارز يراه هؤلاء أعداء الله تعالى أو من قد يشاركهم في ذلك من المسلمين.

These *fatwa* s must be posted, translated, in the companies in which unbelievers are. Sheikh al-$^{c}$Uthaymin's *fatwa* is translated ... available. It has arrived? Good! Here it is, translated, praise be to God. So, it is available translated. Therefore, it [ought to be] posted in the companies and establishments. It is not enough [to do] this, rather it will be posted ... this is available in the Consciousness Raising Office which is here, for those who do not have [it] O Brothers ... ? Orders [should be] posted ... governmental orders ... which prohibit the holding of the like of these celebrations. But, that is not enough [either]. We demand new orders. We demand of th[ose] responsible, these days, new regulations. They are to be translated, posted, and authenticated by governmental seal in all [governmental] bureaus and in all companies. There may be among those present an official, or we must inform them, each one of us in his own way, that this must be done. Those who work in these companies have an even greater duty: that they talk to the authorities and write, through means ... official accepted channels ... and ask for previous instructions, or if there are none available, for new instructions which put an end to this. They [should be] translated according to the language of the people, I mean we have nonbelievers (all refuge is in God) of all races. So, no one will tell you: "I'm German," or English, or French, or -- I don't know -- English. They are to be translated as best we can, according to the companies, and posted on the doors and places ... any prominent place where these enemies of God, may He be exalted, or whatever Muslims might participate in that can see them.

## Selection 6

كذلك الصحافة . وأظن موجود الآن بلا ريب الإخوة مندوبي الصحف . ومنهم الصحافة أو الصفحات الإسلامية . فيجب أن يُكتب وتكرر الكتابة في هذه الأسابيع الباقية عن هذه الأعياد الكفرية . وتبين هذه الأحكام بالتفصيل فيقرأها قطاع كبير من الناس بإذن الله تعالى .

Similarly [we should use] the press. I think, without doubt, [some] newspaper reporter brothers are now present, and among them [there must be those working for] the Islamic press or newspapers. So, these infidel holidays must be written about and th[at] writing [must] be repeated during these remaining weeks. These judgements [must] be explained in detail, so a large sector of the people can read them, with God's permission -- may He be exalted.

## Selection 7

كذلك يجب أن يعلن في الإذاعة . كذلك يجب أن يعلن في التلفاز — بأي وسيلة ممكنة من العلماء وغيرهم . بل يجب أن ننبه علماءنا الكرام إلى أن يجددوا فتاواهم وأن يجددوا التحذير وأن يكتبوا أيضا بمن يهمه الأمر بهذا الشأن بزيادة التجديد . لأنهم كما تعلمون علماؤنا أثابهم الله في كل رمضان يعلموننا أحكام الصيام في كل حجّ يعلموننا أحكام الحج وبدع الحج أو بدع الصيام والصلاة هكذا يعني كل شئ في وقته . فوقت هذه المواسم التي يحتفل فيها الكفار أيضا ينبغي أن نجدد البلاغ والإنذار والتحذير لهؤلاء ونذكر المسلمين بها حتى لا يؤخذوا على غرّة . أيضا يجب أن يعاقب من تسوّل له نفسه أن يتعدى هذه الأوامر . يعني لو علقت الإعلانات فجاء أحد يوزع كروت أو يبيعها فيجب أن يعاقب بعقوبة رادعة لأن هؤلاء قوم لا ينفع معهم إلا الزجر والردع . وهذا من أوجب ما يجب على من بيده المسؤولية بأن الله سبحانه وتعالى قال << الذين إن مكنّاهم في الأرض أقاموا الصلاة وأتوا الزكاة وأمروا بالمعروف ونهوا عن المنكر >> وهذا من أعظم المنكر بلا ريب كما سمعنا في الأدلة .

Similarly, it must be announced on the radio. Similarly, it must be announced on the television -- by any means by scholars and others! Indeed, we must alert our honorable scholars to renew their *fatwa*s, to renew [their] warning, and also to write to those in whom authority in this matter resides even more insistently. Because, as you know, our scholars (may God reward them) -- during Ramadhan -- teach us the rules of fasting. During every ... ahh pilgrimage [season], they teach the rules of pilgrimage and about the things forbidden during Pilgrimage or the things forbidden during fasting and prayers. Just so, I mean, everything [comes] at its [proper] time. So [at] the time of these seasons, during which the nonbelievers celebrate, we also ought to revive preaching, warning, and cautioning against these [people], and [we ought to] remind Muslims about them so they not be caught unawares. It is also necessary that any one who allows himself to be seduced into violating these rules be punished. That means, if notices are posted and someone comes along distributing cards or selling them, he must be strongly punished because these are a kind of people with whom only rebuke and restraint suffice. This is among the greatest of duties for he who bears responsibility because God, may He be magnified and exalted, said: "Those who, if We establish them In the land, establish prayer and give charity, and enjoin the right and forbid wrong."* And, this is, without doubt, the greatest of wrongs, as we have heard in the evidence.

* Qur'an 22:41.

## Selection 8

كذلك يجب على الرقابة الإعلامية أن تسحب كل الكروت والبطاقات — بطاقات التهاني -- من المكتبات وأن تتلف وتحرق ويؤخذ عليهم التعهد الشديد بعدم بيعها مرة أخرى . كما يجب على إدارة الجمارك أو أي جهة مسؤلة في موانئ المملكة البرية والبحرية ألا تسمح بدخول هذه البطاقات والكروت مرة أخرى . بحيث نأتي إن شاء الله في الأعوام القادمة فلا نجد في كتاب الإحصائيات ذكراً لهذا. ما هو ما نجد ذكر يعني تركوا ما يذكروه . لا ! يعني بمعنى أنه حقيقة لم يعد يستورد أي آلة أو أي ذريعة من ذرائع هذه الأعياد الكفرية .

Likewise, Media Censorship must remove all notes and cards -- greeting cards -- from the bookstores, and [those cards must be] destroyed or burned and a serious commitment not to sell them ever again be taken from the [owners of the bookstores]. Similarly, the Customs Bureau (or whatever authority is responsible for the Kingdom's land and sea ports of entry must not allow these notes and cards to enter ever again such that we come (if God so wills) -- in coming years -- not to find, in the statistics book[s], any mention of th[ese cards]. It's not [that] we don't find any mention..., I mean [that] they've left them out [and] not mentioned them. No! I mean in the sense that, in fact, no instrument, nor any medium, of these infidel holidays is any longer imported.

## Selection 9

أمر آخر لابد منه أن يعمم على السفارات وعلى القنصليات والبعثات والهيئات التي تظن أنها بحصانة -- وليس لأحد حصانة أن يعصي الله تبارك وتعالى ويرتكب ما حرم الله -- ويعمم عليها ويطلب منها أن تعمم على أفرادها -- مثل ما يعمم عنهم موضوع اللباس والمطاوعة ومنتبهون له إلى آخره ( هذا أهم وأولى وأوجب ) --أن يعمموا ويقول لهم لا تجاهروا . هذا مخالف . وهو لا شك يا إخوان أن إقامتها ... أن إقامتهم لعيدهم -- لأعيادهم -- علانية ومشاركة المسلمين فيها ورفعهم الصلبان وما يتعلق بهذا هي أشد حرمة من الاختلاط أو من التبرج لأن ذلك يتعلق بالعقيدة . فهذا أمر خطير . ونحن نحارب الكل -- كل الكبائر وكل المنكرات . لكن مجرد أنه يمشي في السوق وتمشي في السوق وشعرها مكشوف أشد منه أنها تكون في حفل عيد ميلاد ويجتمع عندهم المسلمون مع أنها قد يصحب ذلك -- وهذا معروف عندهم -- أنه الخمر والرقص ويعني الزمر والزنا والفواحش . كلها لا يبالون بها وحسبكم أنهم يجتمعون لشعيرة من شعائر دينهم وأنهم يشربون الخمر ! فماذا تتوقع من كافر يشرب الخمر ويخالطهم ما يخالطهم من المسلمين ؟ توقع بعد ذلك كل موبقة ! نسأل الله العفو والعافية . هذا بعض الحلول ولا شك أن الإخوان الكرام لا يفوتهم غيرها وإنما هذا تنبيه .

Another thing, from which there is no escape, is to publicize among the [foreign] embassies, consulates, missions and establishments who imagine that they have [diplomatic] immunity -- no one has any immunity to disobey God (may He be blessed and exalted) and to do what God has forbidden -- to publicize among them and demand of them that they publicize among their personnel -- just as they publicize among them [rules] on the matter of dress and obedience and paying attention to [those things] and so on (this is more important , of higher priority, and higher duty) -- to publicize and tell th[eir personnel] not to behave so publicly. This is a contravention [of law]. It is ... there is no doubt, O brothers, that holding them ... that their holding their holiday -- their holidays -- publicly, and Muslims participating in them and holding up crosses, and things associated with it is more sharply prohibited than mixing [men and women] or the display [of a woman's beauty] because th[e former] is related to doctrine. This is a serious matter. We will fight against the whole -- all crimes and sins. But, the mere fact that he walks in the market place or she walks in the market place, her hair uncovered, more serious than that is that she be at a Christmas holiday party and that Muslims get together with them despite [the fact that there] might accompany [being with them] -- and this is usual with them -- liquor, dance -- I mean -- music, adultery, atrocities. All of that, they do not care about it. Suffice it to say that they get together for one of their religious ceremonies, and they drink liquor! So, what would you expect from an infidel who is drinking liquor, and those Muslims who [are so inclined to] mix with them [do] mix with them? Expect every [kind of] mortal sin! We ask God [for] forgiveness and protection. These are some solutions, and there is no doubt that [you] honorable brothers will not miss others. However, this is just an alert.

## Part 2

### **"Twelve Points"** from ***The True Promise and the False One*** by **Safar al-Hawali**

#### Selection 0

بقي أن نختم بماذا يجب علينا؟ بعد أن رأينا وعد الله تبارك وتعالى الحق وعلمنا أن ما يدعيه الآخرون هو وعد كاذب مزيّف وعرفنا -- بإجمال شديد -- ماذا يريد الأعداء من هذه المشروعات إذاً بقي ماذا يجب علينا أن نعمل؟ وأعتذر إليكم أنني يعني وضعت بعض النقاط على عجل وبديهية وأعترف لكم أن أي واحد منكم في إمكانه إن شاء الله أن يضع مثلها وأفضل منها لأننا نعيش واقع الدعوة على ما فيه من ضعف ولكنه يحظونا الأمل والثقة في الله تبارك وتعالى . وقد رأيت بعض هذه الحلول التي يمكن للدعوة الإسلامية أن تتّخذها وهي موضع نقاش وشورى كما قال الله تعالى << وأمرهم شورى بينهم >>

It remains for us to conclude with "what should we do?" After we have seen God's promise (may He be blessed and exalted), the Truth; and [after] we have learned that what the "others" have been claiming is a false, fabricated promise, and [after] we have come to know -- in [its] stark totality -- what the enemies want out of these projects, then there remains: "what must we do?!" I apologize to you that I have, I mean, set out a few points in a hurry and intuitively, and I give you the excuse that any one of you has the ability, God willing, to set down the likes of [my suggestions] or [even something] better than [I have] because we are [all] living [through] the reality of the *da'wah* despite the weakness of it. But, hope and confidence in God, may He be blessed and exalted, graces us. You have seen some of these solutions which the Islamic *da'wah* can take up. They are a subject of discussion and consultation as God, may He be exalted, said: "And their business is by consultation among themselves."*

* Qur'an 42:38.

## Selection 1

أولاً نشر الوعي العقدي في الأمة قاطبة أن ننشر العقيدة الصحيحة
على الأمة في جميع مستوياتها المثقفين والعامة في جميع الطبقات
الاجتماعية ولاسيما عقيدة الولاء والبراء ونعلن إسلامية المعركة بكل
قوة . مؤتمر مدريد مثلا هذا المؤتمر كغيره من المؤتمرات لم يمثل فيه
الأسلام لم يُقل فيه « قال الله» ولا « قال رسول الله » ولم يُقل فيه
« إن القدس أرض إسلامية .» إذاً هذه قضيتنا الأساسية نحن لا
ننظر إلى الجدل العقيم في النتائج والتوقعات ننظر إلى أساس
القضية . القضية إسلامية دينية لا تخص فلسطينيين ولا العرب ولا
حتى المسلمين المعاصرين اليوم بل هي قضية إسلامية تهم كل المسلمين
إلى قيام الساعة . هكذا يجب أن نعلن المعركة والقضية بوضوح .

First, to extend creedal consciousness throughout the community all together. That we spread the true faith is incumbent upon the community in all its [social] classes: the educated, the common folk -- throughout all social levels, especially the doctrine of loyalty and freedom. And, we shall declare the Islamicness of the struggle with all [our] strength! The Madrid Conference, for instance. This Conference is like every other conference! Islam is not represented at it! [The words] "God said" has [never] been uttered at it! Nor has "God's Prophet said." "Jerusalem *is* Islamic land" has not been uttered at it! Therefore, this is *our* fundamental issue. We are not looking to sterile debate for results and expectations; we look at the root of the issue. The issue is Islamic, religious! It does not concern the Palestinians, nor the Arabs, nor even the contemporary Muslims of today. Rather, it is an Islamic issue which will concern all the Muslims until the End of the World. Thus must we declare the struggle and the issue clearly to be.

## Selection 2

ثانيا إحياء رسالة المسجد . لماذا؟ وهو جزء من الأول لمقاومة هذا
التيار الإعلامي والثقافي الجارف نحن ما عندنا إلا المسجد والحمد لله
أن تأثيره كبير ويجب أن نستفيد منه فنقاوم هذا الغزو عن طريق
الأقمار الصناعية وغيره بهذا الذي في أيدينا ونملكه والله تعالى يبارك
في الجهد القليل ويجعله كثيرا.

Second, to revive the mission of the mosque. Why? It is part of the first [solution]: to resist this raging media and cultural flood, we have only the mosque. Praise God that its effect is great. We must take advantage of it. We will resist this aggression by satellite and other means, by [using] that which is at hand and [that which] we possess. God will bless [our] tiny effort and make it great.

## Selection 3

ثالثا يجب توحيد صفوف أهل السنة والجماعة في جميع أنحاء العالم ليكون ذلك مقدمة لتوحيد صفوف الأمة كلهاعلى منهج السلف الصالح بإذن الله وأول خطوة تكون توحيد أهل السنة والجماعة . المبدأ واحد والمنهج واحد والحمد لله . فلماذا يظلون مشتتين واليهود والنصارى والشرق والغرب كله يجتمع ؟ يجب أن يلتقوا على مناهج عملية ودعوية واضحة لنشر هذه العقيدة لا نقول لتغيير أنظمة الحكم كما يدجّل الدجالون . لا نقول من أجل أن يرفعوا السلاح في وجوه الناس . نحن نقول يجب أن يجتمعوا لنشر العقيدة الصحيحة والدعوة الصحيحة ثم بعد ذلك إذا قامت الحجة ... من قاومها فإن الله سبحانه وتعالى سوف ينصرنا عليه . ومن رضي بها فهذا الذي نأمله في أكثر هذه الأمة والحمد لله . ال ... اجتماع أهل السنة والجماعة ضرورة لوجودهم هم بالدرجة الأولى قبل أن يكون موجها ضد أي أحد آخر كما يفترض البعض وإنما هو ضرورة لإحياء السنة وحفظ كيانهم من الذوابان والضياع في ظل هذه الأوضاع الثقافية الجديدة ومحاربة البدع والشركيات والضلالات والخرافات هي التي تمهّد وتوطن الناس على الكفر بالدجال وخرافات الدجال . ما يؤمن بالدجال إلا الخرافيون -- الذين يؤمنون بالخرافات ويعتقدونها . فلابد من إحياء هذه العقيدة الصحيحة ومنهج السلف الصالح من خلال تعاون وثيق بين أهل السنة والجماعة .

Third, the ranks of the *ahl al-sunnah wal-jama*ᶜ*ah,** in all parts of the world, must unite, so that [unity] may be a prelude to uniting the ranks of the entire *ummah*† in the manner of [our] worthy ancestors with God's permission. The first step will be to unite the people of the Sunnah and *jama'ah*. The principle is one, and the program is one, praise be to God, so why do they remain fragmented while the Jews and the Christians, the West and the East -- all of them, are uniting?

They must come together on clear, practical, missionary programs to spread this faith. We don't say: "to change systems of government" as the imposters do; we don't say [this] so that they shove weapons in people's faces. We say: "[Muslims] must get together to spread the true doctrine and the true call [to faith]." Then, after that, when the truth has arisen ... whoever resists it, God, may He be magnified and exalted, will aid us against him. And, whoever accepts it, well, that is what we hope for in most of this community. Praise be to God. The ... ahh ... the people of the Sunnah and *jama$^{c}$ah's* coming together is necessary for their very existence, in the first place, before it is directed against anyone else, as some prescribe. Indeed, it is necessary to revive the Sunnah and to protect its existence against being absorbed and lost in these new cultural circumstances. Fighting against heresies, polytheistic tendencies, going astray, and superstitions are what will prepare and accustom people to the *dajjal* 's‡ blasphemy and superstitions. Only the superstitious believe in the *dajjal*, those who believe in superstitions and have confidence in them. So, [we] must revive the true doctrine and [our] worthy ancestors' manner through sound cooperation among the people of the Sunnah and Jama$^{c}$ah.

* This is the common phrase used by majoritarian Muslims to describe themselves and to distinguish themselves from Shi$^{c}$i Muslims. It is literally "the people of the 'path' [of the Prophet] and of 'consensual collectivity.'" The last term refers to the Prophet's statement, "my community will never consent to/agree upon [ يُجمعون ] error" and to the concept in Islamic law of إجماع "consensus." We usually reduce the phrase "the people of the *sunnah* and *jama$^{c}$ah* " to "Sunni Muslims" or "Sunnis."

† The Arabic term أمّة indicates the whole of the Islamic "community."

‡ The Arabic term دجّال refers properly, as below, to the "anti-Christ" or false Messiah who will appear at the end of time, but it is widely used, as here, to excoriate any imposter or liar.

## Selection 4

وبالتالى يجب أن نتجنب إثارة الخلافات الاجتهادية أو تعميقها بين
مجموعات أو بين علماء أهل السنة والجماعة . هذه اجتهادات تحل
بطريقة التفاهم وبطريق المودة والمحبة وفيما بينهم دون أن يعرضوها
أو يكشفوها على جمهور الناس . وإذا ابتدأ طرف من الأطراف مخدوعا
أو مغفلا أو مسيّرا بالهجوم على أهل السنة والجماعة فعليهم أن
يسكتوا وأن يصبروا وأن يتحملوا وأن لا يردوا أبدا . حتى لا يزيد في
شغل الأمة بهذا يصبروا وينتقلوا هم إلى المرحلة الاخرى . وأولئك
سوف يتناساهم الزمن بإذن الله وسوف تعلم الأمة ولو بعد حين أنهم
كانوا يخدمون أغراضا لأعدائها وهم قد لا يشعر بعضهم

Furthermore, we must avoid stirring up, or deepening, interpretive* differences between groups or scholars of the people of the sunnah and jama$^{c}$ah. These interpretive endeavors are resolved through understanding and by love and compassion and [are to be resolved] among them without them displaying th[ose differences] or exposing them to the public at large. If some party -- being tricked, or duped or controlled -- starts an attack against the people of the sunnah and jama$^{c}$ah, the[ latter] must be calm, patient, tolerant, and not -- ever -- reply. In order that [such an attack] not increase the community's preoccupation with this [kind of dispute], the[ scholars should] be patient and move on to the next stage. Those [who attack the people], ... "Time" will forget them, with God's permission], and the community will know, even if it should take some time, that they were serving the aims of its enemies, even while some of them might have been unaware of it.

* The term اجتهاد, here used adjectivally, refers to the interpretive procedure by which God's law is derived from the Qur'an and Sunnah of the Prophet by Muslim jurists.

## Selection 5

الخامس فيما أرى ضرورة إنشاء المصارف الإسلامية لمقاومة الاجتياح
الربوي اليهودي الذي يريد أن يجتاح المنطقة . لابد من إقامة مصارف
إسلامية وقد بشرنا سماحة الشيخ عبد العزيز بن باز حفظه الله بأنه
سيصدر إذن إن شاء الله بإقامة بنوك إسلامية في هذه البلاد . وهذا

إن شاء الله كما يعني وعدنا سوف يعلن قريباً إن شاء الله . وإذا تم هذا فهو خطوة يجب أن نفكر جديا فيها. والوقت ليس وقتها وإلا كان أعطيت بعض النقاط الضرورية حتى لا يساء فهم هذه القضية.

The fifth, as I see it, is the necessity of establishing Islamic banks to resist the usurious, Jewish flood which seeks to overwhelm the region. Islamic banks must be established. Sheikh Abdul-[C]Aziz Ibn Baz, may God protect him, has given us the good news that he will issue permission, should God so will, to establish Islamic banks in this country. This, should God so will (as ... I mean ... he promised us), will be announced soon, God willing. If this happens, it will be a step about which we will have to think seriously. The time is not [yet] right, otherwise I would have given you some necessary points [about it] so that an understanding of the issue not be damaged.

## Selection 6

ستة التنبه الشديد لخطر تغيير متدرج للمناهج الدراسية . يعني يتنبه ... أكثر الدعاة يعملون في قطاع التدريس يجب أن يتنبه تغيير المناهج . لا يستغل تغيير أنظمة التعليم وطرق التعليم في تغيير المناهج فتحذف بعلم أو بدون علم المقاطع المعينة التي تشير إلى اليهود يجب علينا أن نتنبه لهذا بل نعوض ونزيد أيضا عندما تشرح أو تفسر ... يعني الأحاديث أو الأيات المتعلقة باليهود أن يزداد يعني فهم الطلاب لها بناء على هذا الواقع .

Six, sharp awareness of the danger of gradually changing educational curricula. I mean, most preachers [must] be aware ... those working in the field of education ... must be aware of changing curricula. Changing systems of instruction and methods of education should not be exploited such that, knowingly or unknowingly, particular sections which refer to the Jews be omitted. We must be aware of this. Indeed, [we must] also compensate and go further when *hadith*s and [Qur'anic] verses, relating to the Jews I mean, are explained or commented upon [so] that students' understanding of them might increase in accord with this reality [we face].

## Selection 7

سابعا يجب أن نبعث الأمل في الأمة بالوعد الحق . لابد من أن نؤمن بالوعد الحق الذي وعده الله تبارك وتعالى ونقرن ذلك بالأدلة الشرعية والواقعية حتى لا تيأس الأمة . فنحن الأمة التي لا تعرف اليأس أبداً ... أبداً في أي مرحلة من مراحل تاريخها . ونحن على ثقة بأن الله تعالى سينصرنا بإذنه تعالى مهما طال الزمن << ولينصرنّ الله من ينصره >>

Seventh, we must revive hope, in the community, regarding the "True Promise." We must believe in the True Promise which God, may He be blessed and exalted, made and yoke it to legal and actual evidence so the community does not despair. We are a community which has not come to know despair, ever ... ever ... in any one of its history's stages. We have confidence that God, may He be exalted, will give us the victory, with God's permission, however long it might take: "God will make victorious he whom He makes victorious."*

* Qur'an, 22:40.

## Selection 8

ثامنا تنشيط الدعوة في الغرب عامة وأمريكا خاصة ورصد تحركات وخطط المتآمرين هناك . وأنا أوجه هذا أولاً لإخواننا المسلمين المقيمين في الغرب وثانيا لنا هنا . تتبعوا هذه الحركات جيدا . أولا تمسكوا بدينكم . وثانيا ادعوا إليه الأمريكان وغيرهم . الأمريكان رغم ما ذكرنا يا إخوان مؤهّل عدد منهم -- ملايين -- إلى أن يدخلوا في الإسلام نتيجة الضياع الفراغ مع الحرية الدينية المعطاة والمتاحة لهم . لو استطاع المسلمون أن يملكوا شبكات تلفزيونية يمكن أن يفعلوا ذلك بنفس الحجة التي يحتج بها أولئك . لاحظوا أن أمريكا تختلف عن بريطانية . تختلف عن فرنسا . ونحن لا نزكيها بل هي والله إنها أعدى عدو نراه في هذه الأرض لكن للحقيقة نقوم المجتمعات تقويما كما أمر الله << إن الله يأمر بالعدل والإحسان >> << إذا قلتم فاعدلوا .>> بريطانيا وفرنسا وغيرها تعادي المسلمين بما يسمى << طرد الملونين >> ... منع الهجرة . حتى منعوا الحجاب . منعوا طفلة مسلمة أن تضع

الحجاب على شعرها . هذا لا يمكن في أمريكا في ظل هذا الدستور الحالى . لا يمكن . لماذا ؟ لأن دستور أمريكا أصلا يقوم على فصل الكنيسة عن الدولة . ويقوم على أن الدين لا يمكن أن تتدخل فيه الدولة أبداً . يعني — معنى آخر — الحكومة الأمريكية بما أنها حكومة لا يمكن أن تنفق ولا دولارا واحدا لانشاء مدرسة دينية . لكن الذي عليها من واجب نحو الدين أنها تعطي المجال لكل طائفة دينية أن تبني ما تشاء من مدارس وتعفي هذه المدارس من الضرائب وتعتبر ما يصرف على هذه المدارس كأنه يُدفع إلى الخزينة العامة للدولة . يعني بدلاً ما نجمع الضرائب من المواطنين ونبني مدارس دينية ندخل في مشاكل مع الطوائف قالوا لا . أي مبلغ يصرف على المدارس الدينية أو الكنائس الدينية أيا كان نوع العبادات فهو جزء كأنه يعطي الدولة . إذاً الطائفة التي تعمل أكثر بنفسها لدينها ينتشر دينها أكثر . ولا يتوقع أن يتغير هذا الدستور الأمريكي قريبا لأن مشاعر الأمريكيين كله متعلقة بوجوده . ما أتوقع أن يتغير. فلو أن المسلمين قووا في أمريكا ونشطوا لاستطاعوا أن يستغلوا هذا وخاصة كما أشرت مع وجود الكاثوليك المنشقين عن الأراء هذه ومع وجود أيضا اليهود المنشقين يمكن عن طريق هؤلاء جميعا إيجاد الخلخلة في هذه الامبراطورية الشيطانية الخبيثة . أكبر إمبراطورية شيطانية في التاريخ هي هذه الولايات المتحدة الأمريكية .

Eighthly, to activate proselytizing in the West in general, and in America especially, and to keep an eye on the activities and plans of conspirators [against us] there. I address this, in the first place, to our Muslim brothers living in the West and, secondly, to ourselves, here. Follow these activities well. First, hold on to your religion, and secondly, call Americans and others to it. Americans, despite what we said [earlier] O brothers, [are] open -- a number of them (millions) -- to accepting Islam as a result of the loss and emptiness [they feel], in spite of the religious freedom given and permitted to them. If Muslims could own TV networks, they would be able do that* by [using] the same line of argument by which those [Christian evangelists] vindicate themselves. Notice that America differs from Britain; it differs from France. We are not praising it. Rather, it is, by God, ... it is the most aggressive enemy that we see on this earth. But, for [the sake of] truth, we [must] assess societies fairly as God ordered [us] to do: "God commands [us] [to do] justice and the good."† "When you speak, speak justly."‡ Britain, France, and others act hostilely toward Muslims by what they call "expelling colored [people]" ... preventing immigration. They've even forbidden the *hijab* . They've forbidden a Muslim girl to put the *hijab* over her hair. That is not possible in America under the protection of [the] current constitution. It's not possible. Why? Because America's constitution, fundamentally, is based on the separation of church from state. [The constitution] is based on [the principle] that religion, ... the state cannot interfere with it, ever. I mean -- in other words -- the American government, although it is a government, cannot spend one dollar to build a religious school. But, that which is its duty to religion is that it must give the chance to all religious sects to build as many schools as they want; to exempt those [religious] schools from taxes, and to consider that which is spent on these schools as if it were paid to the state's public treasury. I mean, [they say to themselves]: "Instead of us collecting taxes from the citizens, building religious schools, and getting into problems with the [various religious] sects," ... they said: "No! " Any amount spent on religious schools or churches, whatever the kind of worship, is a part ... it is as though it were given to the state. Therefore, the sect that works harder for its religion, ... its religion will spread more. This American constitution is not expected to be changed soon because the sentiments of all Americans are bound up with its existence. It is not expected to be changed. So, were Muslims to become strong in America, and become active, they would be able to exploit this. Especially, as I have indicated, with the presence of Catholics rejecting these ideas, and also the presence of break-away Jews, it is possible (through all these) to create a convulsion in this devilish, vile empire. The greatest devilish empire in history is this "United States of America."

* I.e. convert millions of American Christians to Islam.

† Qur'an 16:90.

‡ Qur'an 6:152.

## Selection 9

تاسعا الوقوف بكل قوة — وقوف حقيقي ما هو بيانات — مع الشعب المسلم داخل الأرض المحتلة وإمداده بالمال وقبل ذلك إمداده بالدعوة وبالكتب وكل ما يحتاج إليه في جهاده والحرص على بقائهم في الأرض المحتلة وعلى زيادة عددهم لأن هذا هو الذي يفقد إسرائيل توازنها ويفقدها أعصابها . ولابد أن نعمل على ذلك . إذا فتحت قنوات

بالمنطقة فيجب أن تستغل هذه القناة لهذا الشئ . ما فُتحت عن طريق أمريكا ؟ لماذا الأمريكان بالملايين — ملايين ؟ بالمليارات — يتبرعون لدولة اليهود؟ ونحن — عدد المسلمين في أمريكا خمسة ملايين تقريبا وفي أروبا عدد كبير أكبر من هذا . لماذا لا يصل إليهم يعني الذي يحمل جنسية أمريكية وهو مسلم يستطيع أن يحمل ما يشاء من المال ويدخل إسرائيل كما يشاء لأنه أمريكي أو إنجليزي أو أياً كان . فلماذا لا يستفيد المسلمون من هذا؟ وينسق بينهم هناك وبيننا هنا فيعطون المساعدات والتبرعات ويحملونهم إلى هناك . وكثير من اقتراحات التي لا أحصرها الآن في شئ معين .

Ninthly, standing with all [our] force -- really standing, not [just] declarations -- by the Muslim people within the "Occupied Land" and supplying them with money and, before that, providing them with proselytizing and books and everything they are in need of in their *jihad*. And, taking a concern for their remaining in the "Occupied Land" and to increasing their number because that is what will make Israel lose its balance and lose its nerves. We must work at that. If channels open in the region, we must exploit that channel for this purpose. What has been opened through America? Why do Americans by the millions -- millions!? By the billions they donate to the Jews' state!* And we ..., the number of Muslims in America is about five million, and in Europe it is a large number, larger than this [five million]. Why do [such donations] not reach the[ Palestinians]. I mean, he who has American citizenship, being a Muslim, can carry whatever money he wants and enter Israel just as he wants to because he is an American -- or an English (citizen) or whatever. So, why do Muslims not take advantage of that? [They could] coordinate among themselves there, and with us here, and give assistance and donations and carry them over there.† And, [there are] many suggestions which I will not now limit to any specific thing.

* Notice the ambiguity in the Arabic here. Logically, Americans give billions of dollars; it's not "Americans by the billions give donations," but the distinction is not clear in the Arabic.

† Such activity has occurred, and both the U.S. and Israeli governments are trying to find ways to stop it.

## Selection 10

عاشرا المطالبة بسحب كل الأموال والأرصدة من بنوك هؤلاء الأعداء وصرفها على حاجات الأمة الضرورية في أنحاء العالم الإسلامي إذ كيف يعيش هؤلاء المجرمون — أعدائنا هؤلاء المؤمنون بالمسيح الدجال — يعيشون على مليارات نضعها أرصدة عندهم بينما نحن هنا الملايين من المسلمين يموتون جوعا وفقراً وتشريداً وذلاً. لابد من مطالبة بهذا الشئ وإلا أين السلام وأين حقوق الناس التي يزعمون.

Tenth, calling for the withdrawal of all monies and balances in the banks of these enemies and spending it on the community's vital needs, to the ends of the Islamic world. For, how can these criminals -- these enemies of ours, believers in the false Messiah -- live off the billions which we have deposited with them while we, here -- millions of Muslims, are dying of hunger, poverty, banishment, and humiliation. This thing must be demanded. Otherwise where is "peace?" And, where are the "human rights" which they claim?

## Selection 11

الحادي عشر يجب علينا يا إخوان محاربة الترف والإسراف الذي تعيشه هذه الأمة — والفراغ — وحشد كل طاقات الأمة لمواجهة هذا العدو الأخطبوطي الحقود. وفروا من مرتباتكم من نفقاتكم. أوصوا الأمة بهذا أن توفر طاقاتها وأوقاتها وجهودها لأنها أمام عدو ضخم شرس قد يأتي يوم من الأيام فيسقطنا بالكلية. المعركة يا إخواني أحذر هذه الأمة المعركة ليست معركة غالب ومغلوب. المعركة معركة موجود أو غير موجود. معركة وجود. يراد أن تُمحى هذه الأمة محوا كليا وتصبح عبد العبيد كما قالوا. كنعان عبد العبيد وصفه عبد العبيد عند اليهود والنصارى. لا يعود وجود لنا أبداً.

Eleventh, it is incumbent upon us, O brothers, to combat the luxury and extravagance [in] which the community is living -- and waste --; [we must] mobilize all the community's powers to confront [our] octopus-like, malicious enemy. Save some of your salaries and [save] on your expenses. Advise the community to [do] this, to save its energy [resources], its time, and its efforts because it [stands] before a huge, fierce enemy which may come, one day, to throw us down, totally! The struggle, my brothers -- I am warning this community, the struggle is not a struggle of victor and vanquished! The struggle is one of who is and who is not. A struggle about existence. That this community be totally wiped out and become the slave of slaves, as they have said, is what is wanted. Canaan, the slave of slaves they have described him, the slave of slaves of the Jews and the Christians. No existence is ever to return to us.

## Selection 12

الثاني عشر يجب علينا -- على الدعاة جميعا والخطباء وكل الأمة -- المطالبة بتطوير الجيوش وإعدادها دعويا. وهذا أهم شئ . وتربيتها على الإيمان والجهاد وأيضا علميا بحفز الطاقات المبدعة واكتشاف الإسلحة التي يمكن بها أن نقاوم هذا العدو وألا نركن إلى ما يسمى النظام الدولي الجديد والسلام الذي يريدون أن يفرضوه بحيث لا نحتاج معه إلى جيوش كما يزعمون . ويجب المشاركة أو المساهمة في تصنيع ما يمكن أن نصنع من السلاح . وعندنا التكنولوجية اليابانية . والله ! لو كان عندنا إرادة ! ألآن أعلنوها ! الأمريكان أعلنوها لأن اليابانيين اضطروهم أن يعلنوها ! قالوا إن التكنولوجية التي حاربت في الخليج هي التكنولوجية اليابانية . يعني الأمريكان يضعون مواصفات لاختراع معين . يرسلونه إلى أمريكا ... إلى اليابان فتتسابق الشركات لإنتاجه . ينتجونه ويرسلونه إلى أمريكا . لو كان عندنا إرادة وصدق مع الله وجهاد يمكن أن نضع أي شئ وتنتجه لنا اليابان وغيرها ونتعلم نحن . لكن أقول كمرحلة ممكن أن ينتج مادام المال عندنا والإرادة موجودة ... بهذا المال ... والله أقول إن شاء الله غير آثم . لو عرفنا كيف نستغل الأموال الضخمة التي أعطانا الله إياها -- نحن و دول الخليج -- وابتلانا بها ليرى ماذا نصنع ( لو استطعنا وعرفنا أن نستغلها) -- نستطيع أن نؤثر حتى في الانتخابات الامريكية نفسها . وقد نرشح الرئيس الذي نريد والذي يؤيد ما نريد بناء على المال . وكثير من رؤساء أمريكا يقول نجحت لأنني أعانني ... حتى بوش قال كذا . وغيره يقول أخفقت لأنني كنت لا أمتلك المال اللازم للدعاية . فنحن أموالنا تعطى لمن يفوز. من يفوز المال بين يديه . لماذا لا يكون لنا إسهام في تعيين من يفوز ولو إلى حد ما ؟ هذا فضلا عما يجب علينا بعد ذلك وقبل من خطوات أخرى . وبناء

عليه فأيضا يجب علينا أن نطالب بحفظ ثروات المنطقة -- حفظ
الثروات ( ثروات المنطقة ) -- وفق خطط سليمة تراعي مستقبل
الأجيال القادمة من أبناء المسلمين وأن المعركة قادمة وأن المعركة طويلة
وتراعي حاجات الأمة لا تراعي شركات التطفيف ودول المطففين
العالميين الذين يأخذون خيراتنا بأبخس الأثمان ويصدرونها لنا بأعلى
الأثمان ويخزنونها في مستودعات عندهم تأهبا للمعركة.

Twelfthly, we must -- proselytizers all, preachers and the whole nation must -- demand the development of armies and their preparation in terms of proselytizing. This is the most important thing! And, [we must] educate th[ose armies] in faith and *jihad* as well as scientifically by inciting creative powers and the discovery of weapons with which it will be possible for us to resist this enemy and not have to depend upon what is called the "New World Order" and the "Peace" which they want to impose such that, with the[ose two things], we will have no need of armies, as they claim. Partnershiping or participation in manufacturing those weapons we can make is required. We have Japanese technology. By God! If we only had some will! Just now the Americans announced it. The Americans announced it because the Japanese forced them to announce it. They've said: "The technology which fought in the Gulf War was Japanese technology." That means the Americans set out the specifications of a specific invention. They send it to America ... ahh ... to Japan, and companies will compete to produce it. They make it and send it to America. If we had some will, some fidelity towards God and *jihad,* we could lay out anything, and Japan would produce it for us. Or, others [would], and we would learn. But, I'm [just] saying, as a transitional period, it could be produced as long as we have the money and the will is there ... with this wealth... I swear to God .. I'm saying ... if God wills ... without it being a sin. If we knew how to exploit the huge wealth which God has given us (we, and the Gulf Countries) and by which He has been testing us to see what we make -- if we could and knew how to use it, we would even be able to influence the American elections themselves. We might nominate the president that we want and who would support what we want based on money. Many of America's Presidents say: "I succeeded because [money] supported me." Even Bush said that. And others say: "I was beaten because I didn't have money necessary for advertising." So, our money would be given to the one who would win. Whoever wins, the money would be his. Why couldn't we have some participation in designating who would win, even if only to some extent?* This is over and above what we must do after that and before other steps. Based on th[at], we must demand the preservation of the region's resources -- the preservation of resources (the region's resources) -- through sound plans which will protect the future generations of Muslims' children. [Taking into consideration] that the battle is coming and that the battle will be long, [these plans] will protect the needs of the nation and not protect niggardly companies, and the states of greedy internationalist who take our resources at the cheapest of prices, export them [back] to us at the most expensive of prices, and store them up in their warehouses in preparation of the battle.

* This is particularly interesting in view of allegations about Chinese financial activities in the 1994 U.S. elections. See also "Democratic Fund-Raiser Pursues Agenda on Sudan," *Washington Post* 29 April 1997, A1.

Appendix

# Audience Attitudes

## Introduction

The views of the Saudi Sheikhs are expressed well enough in their lectures *per se,* but what about the attitudes of their listeners? We are able to get some sense of the audience's concerns by listening to their questions. Questions are formally posed, in our sample, only in Sheikh Safar al-Hawali's lecture *A Condemnation of Celebrating Unbelievers' Holidays.* The questions have been submitted, in advance, in writing and are constrained by the topic of the lecture, of course. Nonetheless, they do provide some sense of the audience's perspective. In the following selections, we hear Sheikh Safar read the questions and then respond.

# Appendix

## Q & A

### Selection 1

هذا سؤال — فقد تقرأه — يقول أحد الإخوان فيه << لماذا لا تُسحب هذه المطبوعات ؟>> — و قد أريتكم عشرة نماذج تقريبا منها — << لماذا لا تُسحب هذه المطبوعات وهم يستطيعون أن يسحبوها كما استطاعوا أن يسحبوا جريدة المسلمون في يوم وليلة عندما نشرت << توبة المبحطين ؟>> أنا أقرأ بس . طيب . يعني لو أردنا والله ما شئ . ما في شئ يعجزنا أبداً ( الحمد لله ) في بلادنا . لو استطعنا ... لو أردنا لاستطعنا .

Here is a question -- you might read it -- one of the brothers says in it: "Why are these publications not withdrawn?" I've shown you about ten examples of them. "Why are these publications not withdrawn when the[ authorities] *can* remove [such things], as they were able to withdraw the newspaper *al-Muslimun* within twenty four hours* when it published "The Repentance of the Destroyers"?† I am just reading. Fine. I mean, were we to want [to do so], by God, nothing! There is nothing at all which we can't do (praise be to God) in our [own] country. Were we able ... were we to want [to do it], we could.

* Literally "within a day and a night" indicating one twenty-four hour day.
† I suppose that the reference here is to a specific article, possibly on al-$^{C}$Utaiba and his followers.

### Selection 2

هذا الاخ يقول << أنا أعمل مع أساتذة من الجامعة وخاصة في اللغات الأروبية . وهم يدعون أفراد القسم إلى حفلة من عيد الشكر أو عيد الكريسمس . وبعضهم يصنع شجرة صغيرة يعلق عليها بعض الزخارف . ويأتي بشراب الفواكه ولحم الديك الرومي . >> هالديك الرومي هذا يأكله الأمريكان في عيد الشكر . << هل هذا ... هل عليّ هناك إثم إذا استمريت في العمل بالقسم ؟ >> يجب عليك أن تنكر . ونأثم جميعاً . ما هو أنت وحدك . نأثم جميعًا — من أكبر مسؤل في البلد إلى كل من بلغه هذا الكلام — إن لم ننكر مثل هذا المنكر . يجب علينا جميعاً — كل بحسب استطاعاته — أن ينكر هذا المنكر .

فأول من يجب أن تنكر ... أن تبلغه عميد الكلية . فان لم يسمع فوكيل الجامعة أو مديرها فإن لم يسمع فلتبلغ الإخوان خارج الجامعة ل ... لعل الجامعة يعني ترعو قليلا إن شاء الله .

This brother says: "I work with some professors from the university, especially [some] in European languages. They will invite members of the department to a party for the "Thanksgiving" or the "Christmas" holiday. Some of them set up a small tree, hanging a few decorations on it. They bring in fruit drinks and turkey." (The Americans eat this turkey on the "Thanksgiving" holiday.) "Is this ... Is a sin [counted] against me there if I were to continue* working in the department?" You must disavow [it]. We all sin. Not only you. We all sin -- from the highest official in the country to whomever this word reaches -- if we don't disavow the like of this sin. We must all -- each according to his abilities -- disavow this sin. The first [person] whom you must disavow it [to] ... [whom] you [must] inform is the dean of the College. Then, if he doesn't listen, the university's Trustee or Director. Then, if he doesn't listen, then you are to inform† the brothers outside of the university to ... ahh perhaps the university, I mean, will repent, if God wills.

* Compare the dialectal verb form اسْتَمَرَّيت with the standard اسْتَمْرَرْتُ "I continued."
† Not the use of the particles ف and ل with the jussive mood of the verb تُبَلِّغْ to indicate an indirect imperative.

## Selection 3

يقول الاخ << إن موقف الرسول ( صلي الله عليه وسلم ) عندما جاء المدينة فوجد اليهود يحتفلون بيوم نجّى الله فيه موسى فقال عليه الصلاة والسلام ما معناه نحن أولى منهم بأخي موسى فصام ذلك اليوم وهو عاشوراء فهل نستطيع أن نقف وقفاً مشابهاً لموقف الرسول صلى الله عليه وسلم بالنسبة لعيد النصارى؟ >> ليس في هذا أي دليل على أية حال ولاسيما عند سؤالك عن عيد النصارى . لأن كما أشرنا أولاً النبي ( صلى الله عليه وسلم ) فعل ذلك فما فعله تبعناه ما لم يفعله لن نتبع . ثانيا عيد النصارى محدث حتى في دينهم . لاحظوا أن عيدهم يقترن به اعتقادهم أن المسيح صُلب ورُفع في هذا اليوم . في بعض أيامهم ... أو بعض طرائقهم -- كنائسهم -- تعتقد هذا . ونحن نعتقد -- كما ذكر ربنا( تبارك وتعالى) -- << وما قتلوه وما صلبوه ولكن

شُبّه لهم .>> الأمر الآخر أن صيام النبي ( صلى الله عليه وسلم ) هو غير صيام أهل الكتاب . فهذا صيام وهذا غير ذلك . ثم بعد ذلك — كما تعلمون — نزل صيام رمضان . فعلى الأقل نقول إن هذا يكفي أنه يعني نقتصر على ما ورد ولا نزيد عليه وهذا يكفينا فكل محدثة بدعة وكل بدعة ضلالة مع ما يعارضهم من أدلة كلية وتفصيلية ذكرناها بهذا الشأن . أما يعني من أخذ ... أو فهم منه — كما أسلفنا — أننا نصوم مخالفة لهم فقلنا إن الأولى ألا يكون ذلك لأن الصيام تعظيم فنكون كأننا اشتركنا معهم في تعظيم عيدهم .

Th[is] brother says: "The Prophet's position (may God bless him and grant him peace), when he came to Medina and saw the Jews celebrating the day on which God saved Moses, [was such that he] said: What is the meaning of that?! We are more closely related to my brother Moses than they.' Then he fasted [on] that day, it being ᶜ*Ashura'*. So, can we take a position similar to that of the Prophet (may God bless him and grant him peace) with regard to the Christians' holiday?" There is not, about this, any evidence, in any case, especially on your question about the Christians' holiday. Because -- as we have pointed out -- first of all, the Prophet (may God bless him and grant him peace) did that. And, whatever he did, we have followed; what he didn't do, we will never follow. Secondly, the Christians' holiday is an innovation, even in their religion. Notice that their Holiday ... their belief that the Messiah was crucified and was raised up on that day is associated with [that holiday]. During some of their days ... or some of their sects -- [some] of their churches -- believe that. But, we believe -- as our Lord (may He be blessed and exalted) said: "But they did not kill him, and they did not crucify him. But, so it was made to appear to them."* The other thing is that the Prophet's fasting (may God bless him and grant him peace) is different than the People of the Book's fasting. Th[e former] is one [kind of] fasting and th[e latter] is something else. Then, after that -- as you know, fasting on Ramadhan was revealed. So, at the very least, we [can] say: "It is enough that, I mean, we restrict ourselves to that which has come [to us from God]. We will not add [anything more] to it." That is enough for us. For, every innovation is a heresy, and every heresy is an error, in addition to some comprehensive and [other] detailed proofs that contradict the[ People of the Book] which we have [already] mentioned in this regard. As for he, I mean, who has taken ... or has understood [all this to mean] -- as we have mentioned above-- that we fast for the purpose of being different from them, we say: "The most appropriate [thing] is that that not be [so]" because fasting is a glorification. So, we would be [seen] as participating with them in glorifying their holiday.

* Qur'an 4:156.

## Selection 4

يقول الاخ << ما رأيكم في وسائل الإعلام التي تهتم بأعياد الكفار مثل صحيفة الشرق الأوسط ومجلة المجلة ؟>> هذه على طول تجد فيها << عيد الميلاد >> و << الأعياد . >> وهذه الثانية ... الوسخة هذه ... صباحية ؟ ما أدري اسمها ؟ هذه أكيد بدعي أكثر ... كلها ... والمسائية إلى آخره . كل هذه سوف تكون بل حتى مجلات الأطفال التي تصدر عن هذه المؤسسة وأمثالها تتكلم عن عيد الميلاد هذا دأبهم وهذا شأنهم . الواجب أن ننكر عليهم بما استطعنا . وأقل شئ أننا ننكر على وزارة الإعلام أن تدخل أي مجلة فيها هذا الكلام وخاصة إذا كانت سعودية لأن الناس يعتبرون هذا قدوة . فيجب -- يعني من الآن ... الفرصة أمامنا -- أن ننكر عليهم وأن ننكر ونطالب بعدم دخول أي عدد يُذكر فيه هذه الأعياد وكما ذكرنا في الحلول الأخرى بيع كروت الأعياد ... وهذا ذكرنا أنه حرام وأنه قد يكون كفراً إذا اعتقد صاحبه أن هذا عيد جائز وصائغ وأن دينهم حق ونحن نبيعه كما نبيع بقية الأشياء المباحة فقد يكون كفراً نسأل الله العفو والعافية ويجب أن تُسحب هذه الكروت من جميع المكتبات التي تبيعها .

Th[is] brother says: "What is your opinion of the information media which concerns itself with the unbelievers' holidays like the *Sharq al-Awsat* newspaper and the *Majallah* magazine?" This [first paper] ... always ... you'll find in it [announcements like] "Christmas" and "holidays." This second one ... this dirty [one] ... a morning paper? I don't know its name. This is surely more heretical ...all of them ... and the evening [papers] and so on. All these will exist. No! Even children's magazines which come out of these establishments and their likes talk about the Christmas holiday. This is their habit; this is their business. [Our] duty is to denounce them as much as we can. The least we can do is to rebuke the Ministry of Information for introducing any magazine in which there is this kind of statement, especially if it be Sa'udi [owned] because people will consider it to be an example. So, [we] must --from now on ... the opportunity [stands] before us -- denounce [them] and demand not to [allow] entry to any issue in which these holidays are mentioned. As we have mentioned in [our discussion of] other solutions, the selling of holiday cards ... and we have mentioned that that is forbidden; and that it may be infidelity if their owner believes that [such a] holiday is permissible and legitimate and that their religion is right and that we [may] sell them as we sell other, permissible things ... may be infidelity. We ask God [for] forgiveness and protection. These cards must be removed from all the stores which sell them.

## Selection 5

<< هناك شباب هداهم الله ينتظرون أعياد الكفار للذهاب إليها والتمتع بالرؤية إلى النساء وما يفعلون في هذه الأعياد . فالرجاءإعطاء نصيحة لهم . >> ننصحهم وأنفسنا بتقوى الله تبارك وتعالى وألا نرتدّ كافرين بعد إذ هدانا الله للاسلام وألا نشارك هؤلاء الكفار في شريعتهم وفي شعائرهم كما قد أوردنا وأسلفنا.

"There are some youths, may God guide them aright, who wait for the infidels' holidays to go to them and to enjoy looking at the women and they are doing. So, please give advice to them." We advise them, and ourselves, to fear God; that we not to fall back into being infidels after God has guided us to Islam and that we not join those infidels in their ritual or in their ceremonies, as we have mentioned and alluded to.

## Selection 6

يقول الاخ << كبار المسؤولين في الشركات هم من اليهود والنصارى وبالتالي هم يصدرون تعميم إجازة لهذا اليوم . >> طبعاً ليس كل الشركات كبار المسؤولين فيها يهود أو نصارى لكن يوجد . نعم . يوجد شركات الكبار فيها هؤلاء. وهذا من الحرام . وجود الكفار مسؤولين في بلادنا حرام . إذا كان مجرد من دخولهم إياها حراماً فكيف يكونون أيضاً مسؤولين والموظفون المسلمون تحتهم يتحكمون فيهم ؟ ولذلك لا يجوز لأن يبقوا رؤساء . هذا أولاً مبدئياً. ثم لا يجوز أن يُقر هذا اليوم يوم عطلة أو عيد عطلة لهم . فان كان ولابد ... فكحل انتقالي -- ( وألان ... أنا دائماً — تعرفون-- من أجئ أن أقول لا نرقع المسألة . يجب أن يخرجوا من جزيرة العرب . يجب أن يخرجوا . هذا أمر الله ورسوله . ) لكن كحل انتقالي — لا يجوز

للمسلمين أن يعطلوا ... أن يعيّدوا في هذا . سبحان الله العظيم .
المسلمون إذا جاء الحج يشتكون والله كثير جدا -- في رمضان -- ما
يعطون إجازة للاعتكاف. ما يعطون إجازة للحج ويفوتهم الحِج .
وتُعطى إجازات الشركات في عيد الميلاد حيث يعطل الكفار فيُرغم
المسلمون في بلاد الإسلام على أن يعيّدوا مع الكافرين ويعطلوا مع
الكافرين . نعوذ بالله . هذا والله نحن قد رضينا بالدنية في ديننا
وقد أسأنا إلى المسلمين وأذللناهم إذا أقررنا هذا الأمر فهذا لا يجوز
قطعاً .

Th[is] brother says: "The top officials in companies are Jews and Christians, and furthermore, they issue vacation announcement[s] for this [kind of] day." Of course, not all companies' top officials are Jews or Christians, but [that does] exist. Yes. There are companies in which the big[ shot]s are those [kinds of people]. And, this is religiously forbidden. The presence of nonbelievers, as officials -- in our country, is religiously forbidden. If their mere entering it is religiously forbidden, how can they be officials with Muslim employees under them, issuing orders to them? For that reason, it is not permissible for them to remain chiefs. This is [the] first [thing], as a matter of principle. Then, it is not permissible that [such a day] be set as a day off or a holiday-vacation for them. But if it must be, then ... as a transitional solution -- (Now, I'm always -- you know -- one who comes along to say, "Let's not aggrevate the problem." They must leave the Arabian Peninsula; they must leave. This is an order from God and His messenger), but as a transitional solution -- it is not permissible for Muslims to take a day off ... to celebrate this [holiday] Glory be to God, Most Great. Muslims, when pilgrimage [season] has come, complain, by God very many [complain] -- and during Ramadhan -- they are not given vacation [time] for *'I* [C]*tikaf* .* They are not given vacation for pilgrimage, so the *hajj* passes them by. But, company vacations are given on the Christmas holiday so the unbelievers [may] celebrate, and Muslims be compelled, in the [birth]land of Islam to celebrate with infidels and vacation with infidels. We seek refuge in God! In addition to that, we [will have] accepted the abasement of our religion, and we [will have] abused Muslims and humiliated them if we allow this matter [to continue].† But, this is absolutely impermissible.

* Mosque rituals associated with the final breaking of the fast.

† Notice that the tenses of the verbs are, here, determined by the (*inverted*) conditional sentence structure.